TEN MEN

TEN MEN

A YEAR OF CASUAL SEX

KITTY RUSKIN

ICON

Published in the UK and USA in 2024 by
Icon Books Ltd, Omnibus Business Centre,
39–41 North Road, London N7 9DP
email: info@iconbooks.com
www.iconbooks.com

ISBN: 978-18773-068-1
ebook ISBN: 978-183773-070-4

Typeset in Bell MT by SJmagic DESIGN SERVICES, India.

Printed and bound in Great Britain

CONTENTS

TW: Sexual assault, suicidal ideation

BEFORE THE TEN

At ten years old, I pulled up my jeans and walked away from my first sexual experience.

It felt like everything in my head had been rearranged. One moment, the boy down the street was asking me to be his girlfriend. The next, we were crouching in the bushes at the bottom of a field, and he told me to touch his penis. 'This is what girlfriends do,' he told me.

I tried to get out of it, insisting again and again that I didn't want to.

'Why?' he asked.

I scrambled around for an answer. For some reason, 'I don't want to' didn't seem to be enough.

'Well, what if someone sees?' I shrugged.

'They won't, I promise. No one can see us here.' His tone turned urgent. Dismissive. 'Come on.'

I continued to shake my head, but he refused to take 'no' for an answer. After a few minutes, I decided that I had no choice – I'd do what he asked and get it over with. This turned out to be something close to oral sex. Then he asked me to pull down my trousers and underwear so that he could repeat the act on me.

Buttoning my jeans afterwards, I felt the worst feeling I'd ever felt. The ground beneath my trainers felt strangely unsteady, the trees leaning at funny angles all the way home.

When I got back to my bedroom, every stuffed animal and doll seemed to know what I'd done. How I'd ruined myself with no return. Their faces, once so cheering, now seemed to look away. Getting into bed, I tried to forget it with immediate effect.

But I couldn't. Not entirely. And, without really realising it, I became obsessed with the idea of 'purity' from that day onwards, clutching at mine like a flimsy cardigan the wind was trying to pull away. During the transition from pre-teen to teenager, then teenager to young adult, I grimaced at the thought of kissing strangers and one-night stands, thinking that this represented resilience and lofty morals. Some feminist streak in the face of the hyper-sexualisation of women. I would never be like that, I told myself. I'm not that kind of girl.

The actual source of my disdain was fear, confusion and, above all, shame.

As I entered my early twenties, I began to cotton on to the fact that this rigid attitude was rooted in guilt and anxiety. Finally, I came to terms with the fact that something bad had happened to me years ago. Something which was wrong and that shouldn't have happened. Most importantly, I understood that it was something I no longer needed to feel ashamed of or push down or ignore. I didn't need to bury it. The shame wasn't mine to bear.

I finally realised that the experience had made me sex-averse not, as I once thought, because I was principled, but because I was traumatised.

Moving through this trauma was like walking through mud, each step sinking a little deeper than I had anticipated. The epiphany came, at first, like a light bulb moment; a switch flipped inside my head. I'd been watching a documentary about sexual assault survivors, and unexpectedly found myself relating to their experiences. To the misplaced guilt they felt; to the way they retreated from loved ones; to the black hole of misery that threatened to swallow them up. Feelings of shame had been tormenting me for years, and in the space of a few minutes they dissipated. I realised that, like those people, I had nothing to be ashamed of. I had done nothing wrong. I didn't need to keep the assault a secret anymore.

So I told people close to me, and the relief was incredible. The more I processed, the lighter I felt. In those first few months, sex gradually stopped being a frightening, impure thing. Unfortunately I couldn't afford therapy, but through conversations and self-reflection, I was able to separate sex and shame, sex and fear, sex and secrecy, and started to look at it anew. Far from an ominous threat, sex began to morph into an exciting, tantalising prospect. I had to take it day by day, but as the months passed I felt secure in my newfound attitude.

2018 ended, and as 2019 began, I had one goal, one New Year's resolution: to stop being so precious about who I had sex with. I decided to have sex with as many people as I wanted to. To taste different mouths; to feel different bodies. There would be no more clutching of the pearls.

Coincidentally (or perhaps not), it was during this time that I started binge-watching *Sex and the City*. Samantha became my shining example, with her upturned nose and flicked blonde hair; her hand around a man's tie as she pulled him inside. As Samantha declares in one of her most iconic speeches, I told myself that, from now on, I would blow whomever I chose.

No more guilt. No more self-loathing. No more self-limitation.

It was quite the baptism of fire. I'd only lost my virginity two years prior, and I'd felt very differently about sex back then.

———————◆———————

There had been plenty of tension building up to the night Matt and I slept together (and I finally lost my virginity). Eight years of it, in fact.

I met Matt when I was in Year Nine at school (aged fourteen), locking eyes with him on the other side of the common room. Glancing down at my hot-pink iPod, I quietly filed away his thick, dark curls and yellow-brown eyes, eventually mentioning him to a friend. I tried to sound casual, but she saw right through me.

'He has a girlfriend,' she told me mournfully, and I shrugged off my disappointment. Oh well, I thought. That's that!

Years later, however, I saw on Facebook that he was starting his master's at Edinburgh University at the same time I was. Some quick sleuthing (read: stalking) also revealed that he was single. So, I dropped him a friendly, casual message, my heart in my mouth.

Ten minutes later, Matt replied.

Thus began the pointless ping-pong of messages: 'How are you?', 'How's life?', 'Kept in touch with anyone?' All the questions neither party really wants the answers to, until someone finally plucks up the courage to ask the other person out. At last, Matt asked if I wanted to go to a gin bar near George Square. We spent one night at this bar, the following Friday at a restaurant, and the Thursday after that in an Old Town pub.

He didn't kiss or touch me on any of these dates. But every time I took the bus home, silently concluding that our relationship was platonic, he messaged and asked me out again. For our fourth date, he suggested that we go to an Italian restaurant a stone's throw away from his flat.

We could go back to mine and watch a movie afterwards, he added. I could hear the tentativeness in his voice, even over text.

Go back and watch a movie? I repeated to myself, raising my eyebrows as I looked down at my phone. I may have been a virgin, but I knew what *that* meant.

A week later, we talked about our friends and childhoods over a carbonara, attempting a breeziness which felt forced. I revealed my own anxiety by dropping a knife on the floor with an almighty clang, streaking pasta sauce across a waiter's shoe. He revealed his when the same waiter asked him to tap his card and he tossed it between his hands, eventually dropping it into his lap. The poor man must have been glad to see us go.

When Matt and I finally left the restaurant, it was with a shared nervous energy that was hard to ignore. It hummed beneath our tipsy conversation and quick, sidelong looks.

'This is a nice area,' I said mildly.

'Yeah. Very nice,' he told the pavement. 'No complaints here.'

'Quite far from campus, I suppose?'

'Yeah, true. There's the bus, though.' Matt jabbed a thumb in a vague direction. 'The 21?'

'Oh, yeah. I know it. I think I've been on it once. Can't remember why.'

As we climbed the steps to his stone-grey townhouse, my nerves reached a fever pitch. Did I tell him I was a virgin? I wondered. Could I, at the age of 22, or would he run a mile? Maybe he wouldn't be able to tell. If that was the case, I'd say nothing, I decided, my mouth a straight line.

Heaving open the door, Matt let us in, the sound of our footsteps bouncing around the high ceilings inside.

'Oh, wow. Big in here,' I observed, craning my neck. With a nod, he led me up a set of tiled stairs, rooting around for his key. His face lit up when he finally found it.

'In we go!' Matt exclaimed, holding the key up proudly. I glanced at the back of his head as he unlocked the door, registering how enthusiastic he sounded. Strained, almost.

God, my heart was straining too – desperate to spring out of my chest and patter down the hall. Stepping over the threshold into a boy's flat for the very first time, I looked around the cavernous hallway. More high ceilings, the walls a dull grey; white mouldings at each corner. A muddy bike leant against the wall, and I could hear faint rumblings of a movie from a flatmate's bedroom. This had probably been nice once, I thought. Fancy and Georgian with a piano tinkling away in the living room. It was so studenty now, ghosts probably didn't bother haunting it. The whiskey bottle line-up along the floor was too depressing.

'That's my room, go on in.' Matt pointed to a door at the end of the hall. 'I'll be in in a second.'

Drifting into his bedroom, I took stock of the red candles and white tea lights scattered across his desk and bedside table. Well, he was either attempting romance or about to host a séance, I thought.

Candles aside, it was a pretty bog-standard student room. More high ceilings with chipping wallpaper, along with broken blinds, a flimsy poster, a neglected keyboard and a stack of earmarked textbooks. I was thumbing through one when Matt exclaimed 'So!' from behind me.

'So!' I returned nervously, wheeling round. 'This is, um, a nice room?'

Looking askance, I dropped down onto the bed. I hardly knew what else to say, so thought I'd just keep saying that things were nice. This could only tide me over for so long, I thought with rising panic.

'Thanks,' Matt smiled. God, how was he so calm all of a sudden? Had he taken a shot in the kitchen? When he settled down on the bed, resting back on his elbows and looking at my mouth, I felt my body spring back up like a jack-in-the-box.

'Where's your loo?' I could feel my face pinkening.

'Second door on the left.' Matt reached under the bed and produced a toilet roll. He smiled. 'Bring this back when you're done.'

I looked down at the toilet roll in my hand and nodded, shuffling awkwardly out into the hall. Romance now well and truly dead, I took my toilet roll to a narrow bathroom with no mirror and sat down on the cold toilet seat. For a moment I stayed very still, willing my thoughts to quieten. Closing my eyes, I tried to settle into the black, but the silence was short-lived. Thoughts crowded into my mind, rushing past each other like clouds on a windy day. *Oh God, is this the night?* my scattered brain asked. *Is this the night I finally have sex?*

Tonight could mean so many things … No more lying to my friends about all the phantom sex I said I'd had. No more praying that people wouldn't ask for details when I drank during Never Have I Ever. No more knowingly nodding when a friend was telling me about penises or blow jobs or 69'ing. I was actually going to *see* a penis in person. I was going to find out what sex was really like.

Yes, I was potentially about to lose the chains of my virginity in *that* bedroom down *that* hall. And I wasn't sure how I felt about that. Excited, relieved, overwhelmed ...

Horribly, horribly nervous?

Yeah, I was scared shitless. I wasn't sure, at this point, why sex frightened me so much. My revelation about an earlier trauma hadn't arrived yet – it wouldn't come for years. At this stage, all I had was a sneaking suspicion that the Bad Thing had happened, but I wasn't ready to face up to that suspicion yet. It was far easier, back then, to pin my virginity down to being awkward and frigid. And if my awkwardness was the only thing stopping me from having sex, why couldn't I just push through it? Why couldn't I get it over with?

Having sex certainly seemed like something I should have done by now, I thought miserably. As much as I silently judged the people who slept around, I was ashamed of my virginity; embarrassed by my lack of experience. I was sick and tired of being shut out of conversations, terrified that I'd be discovered if I tried to join in. More than anything, I just wanted to join the club of People Who Had Had Sex. Only then would I become a proper adult and a real woman.

And Matt was nice, right? Safe, kind Matt, who I'd known for years ... why shouldn't I lose my virginity to him? He was a very respectable choice.

With a sigh, I got up to wash my hands, trying to swallow a fresh wave of nausea. That was all very well and good, but if you'd never had sex before, how did you know how to do it?

My face hot, I realised that I wasn't even sure what a penis and ball sack *looked* like. Not in detail, anyway (I'd blocked out the memory of what happened to me at ten). I flashed back to my classmates doodling penises on each other's books in Year Nine. My terror of drawing one wrong.

If I didn't know what a penis looked like, how would I know what to do with it? Sure, I knew in principle about hand jobs and blow jobs, but I'd never practised on a banana, and I'd never watched porn. Oh, why hadn't I watched porn in preparation? I asked the ceiling. Why hadn't I gone to Sainsbury's and bought a bunch of practise bananas?

Shaking my head, I shut off the water, the tap shrieking in protest. What mattered tonight was losing my virginity, I reminded myself. And that was just a case of him putting his penis in my vagina – surely I could manage that. *Surely.* I'd lie back and think of England, as they say.

But what if I bled? a small voice asked. I grimaced, imagining a torrent of red bursting out like water from a dam. His sheets *had* been very white. Oh lord, would he expect me to pay for them? I could hardly afford my own bedspread, let alone someone else's.

And what if the sex was insanely, unbearably painful? another one chimed in. *What if it was the worst pain I'd ever felt? Worse than the time that boy sat on my finger in judo and nearly broke it clean off?*

I gave myself a few moments to calm down. Breathing in deeply (in for eight, out for ten, in for eight, out for ten), I fixed my eyes on the floor and prepared myself like a soldier leaving for battle. No matter how painful, I'd persevere, I told myself. I *would* lose my virginity tonight, come hell or high water.

Slightly green, I returned to Matt's room and handed him back his toilet roll. As I settled down next to him, I registered that every candle and tealight had been lit in my absence. Well, this had better not be a séance, I thought grimly.

'You ready?' Matt asked me.

'For what?' I baulked.

'The movie.' Chuckling, he nodded to the laptop in front of him. 'We said we'd watch *Anchorman 2.*'

'Oh, yeah.' My chuckle was more nervous than his. 'Yeah, sure.'

With another nod, Matt hit the space-bar on his laptop and the movie began.

To my surprise, we didn't just watch some of it – we watched all of it. Not only that, but Matt didn't touch me once. Not once! Not so much as an arm around the shoulder or a squeeze of the knee. Glancing at his profile, I thought, *I don't get it.* Wasn't 'watching a movie' codeword for 'sex'? Had I come all the way across town just to watch *Anchorman 2*?

I fidgeted, my frustration mounting. Was sex going to happen at all tonight?

When the film ended and Matt still hadn't touched me, my nerves shifted into resignation. Well, here it is then, I thought glumly. Another night of no sex. Perhaps I'd misread the entire situation and he really did just want to be friends. Oh, I was an idiot.

'Well, what do you want to do now?' Matt asked when the credits finished, oblivious to my tortured inner dialogue.

I looked away, mocked by the waning light of half-a-dozen tealights.

'Er, I should probably go home. I have a meeting with my tutor in the morning.'

'Oh no! Really?' Matt sat up as if a bolt had run through him, his voice rising in panic. 'No, well, you … you don't *have* to.' His eyes were insistent. 'Why don't you stay the night?'

I considered this for a moment, looking down at his white sheets warily. If I stayed and this became some weird, platonic sleepover, I could sleep more comfortably at home. But I was still a little tipsy and my flat *was* all the way across town. And there might be hope yet …

Well, I might get a kiss, at least.

'Okay,' I smiled unenthusiastically. 'Sure.'

'Great!' Matt settled back onto the bed, his face softening as he looked at me. 'Wait here. I'm just going to go and brush my teeth.'

And with that he shimmied down the mattress and into the hall, the buzz of his toothbrush groaning from the bathroom. Feeling a bit of a lemming, I wondered whether he expected me to brush my teeth as well. I hadn't even thought to bring a toothbrush. Oh dear.

With clean teeth and no trousers, Matt eventually returned. I tried very hard not to blink with surprise when I saw him. There was my old school friend, stripped down to a T-shirt and boxers, all hairy knees and purple socks and a very discernible *bulge*. I felt silly by contrast, sitting there fully dressed. Should I have stripped as well? Was 'cleaning my teeth' code for 'getting undressed'?

Well, I didn't have long to dwell on it.

With a final smile, Matt turned off the light. A moment later he was on top of me, his hands in my hair and his tongue in my mouth.

I blinked in the dark, kissing him back. Okay, okay! So this wasn't a platonic sleepover, after all. I felt a cold rush of both anxiety and relief, feeling around for his hair. This is *really* happening, I thought frenziedly, my heart beginning to pound. Sex is really happening. Right here, right now.

As terrified as I was, I couldn't help noticing how nice it was kissing Matt. I hadn't kissed anyone in a long, long time, and this all felt wonderfully easy. I closed my eyes as he pulled my dress over my head, his fingers fumbling for the clasp of my bra.

For a while it was just writhing around and snogging (very nice). And then:

'Kitty,' Matt said breathlessly between kisses. 'I have a question.'

'Oh yeah?' Now is not the time for talking, I wanted to say, but asked: 'What's up?'

'Well, are you—'

He stopped suddenly, and my heart quickened. Surely he couldn't *tell* I was a virgin? I asked the ceiling anxiously. Surely he couldn't *know?*

'Well,' Matt resumed, lowering his mouth to my ear, 'are you a ... married lady?'

Silence.

'What?' I giggled uncertainly, staring at him in the dark. 'What do you mean?'

'I mean: are you a married lady?'

'No, I'm ... not.' My laughter became unsure. 'Otherwise I wouldn't be doing this, would I?'

Matt's body tensed. Confused, I frowned. According to his body language, 'no' wasn't the answer he wanted. Was this some kind of weird roleplay, then? I wondered. Should I just ... go along with it?

'Er, yes, I'm married?' I ventured.

'I see.' Matt let out a low chuckle, pulling me closer. His body eased, melting around me like butter.

'With ... four kids?'

His chuckle darkened, and I cocked an eyebrow, glad that we were in the dark.

At the time, I didn't consider how weird it was to role-play during our first night together, especially as we'd only just started kissing. For all I knew, this was perfectly normal foreplay.

It was not, however, and sadly, only got weirder from there. I'm not sure what sub-category of porn he'd seen, but soon enough Matt started kissing the length of my body and turning me over, before repeating the process on the other side. He did this again and again. On the fourth turn I felt like a pancake on Shrove Tuesday, flipping about in the pan. By the fifth I was dizzy, confused and struggling to hold in a hysterical bout of laughter. By the sixth I was *sure* he wasn't going to flip me over again, but around and about I went.

Finally, he gave up this strange song and dance, and we returned to kissing. That's better, I chortled to myself. What in God's name was that?

Well, never mind. The kissing was nice, and his hands were nice and, soon enough, I got my first hint of the Main Event. With a small thud, Matt paused to open a draw beside the bed, followed by the crackle of plastic. Here it came, then, I thought, with a flood of nerves. *The condom.* Intercourse was looming, just as Matt was looming over me in the darkness like an enormous bat. Biting down on my lip, I attempted a quick pelvic floor exercise in preparation.

Another panicky thought occurred to me, then: what if he asked me to put the condom on and I couldn't do it? What if I tried to put it on and inadvertently flicked it back into my face? For goodness' sake, why hadn't I practised on a banana?

But to my relief, the gentle rustling that followed suggested he was putting it on himself. It occurred to me then that it might be a good thing I couldn't see his penis, dark as it was. My fourteen-year-old friend Ida (a beautiful, peroxide-blonde Swede) had told me in Year Eight that penises were hideous and that vaginas were much nicer. She was probably right about that, I thought in a measured way, and I didn't want it putting me off.

Latex on, Matt resumed kissing me. Then he ran his hands up my neck and into my hair as he tried to pull himself into me. Oh, fuck, I thought weakly. Here it came!

I sucked in a quick breath, blinking hard. It was a bizarre sensation, and not the one I'd imagined at all. I wasn't in searing pain, but my body seemed to be seizing up below the belt, resisting his penis like it was a battering ram and my vagina was a pair of unyielding doors. He tried to break through again without success, and tried again after that. After the third attempt, the air between us became thick with embarrassment.

We paused for a few, long moments, and then with a cursory kiss on the neck Matt tried again. At last he broke through, and a sharp rush of pain made me bite down on my tongue. Oh, fuck, I thought. But also: hooray! Hooray and ohmyGod: *I had a penis inside me.* A penis inside me! Also: ow.

Biting harder, I gripped Matt's shoulders.

'Sorry, but can we stop?' I winced.

'Oh!'

Horrified, he pulled himself out, and my body almost crumbled with relief.

'Are you okay?' he asked me quietly, resting back on his haunches. I could faintly see his eyes widen with shock.

'Yeah. I'm so sorry.' Now would have been the perfect time to tell him I was a virgin, but instead I said: 'It just hurt a little. I'm sorry.'

'No, don't be sorry!' Matt insisted. I smiled up at his vague outline. Though he was still looming over me, his kindness was reassuring. 'Shall we just ... stop then?'

'Um, yes. If that's alright.'

'Of course it is! Of course ...'

Rolling over to lie beside me, Matt tucked me into his arms. And that's when I felt it: safety, when I lowered my head to his chest, the warmth from his skin mingling with mine. In spite of the flipping (which did, ultimately, earn him the title 'Pancake Man' among my friends), I was grateful for the experience. Grateful to have lost my virginity to someone so patient and understanding.

I was shocked by how easy it was, lying with him like this. How pleasant it was, touching his arms and running a hand over his ribs; brushing his dark hair out of his face and kissing his mouth. Folding my body into someone else's like this wasn't frightening, it was comforting. Like coming in from the rain.

As I listened to his gentle heartbeat under my ear, the sky lightening to a dusty blue outside, I felt another swell of relief rise inside me. Finally, I had confirmation of what I'd only hoped before: that I could have sex without shame.

What a revelation.

———

In spite of all that gratitude, I decided not to see Matt again. I don't think either of us saw our relationship blossoming after that night, so I slipped out the next morning, regurgitating my lie about an early-morning tutor meeting.

'Oh, yeah,' he yawned, his mouth huge and round. 'That's fine. I'm going to get in the shower. You can stay here if you want and we can have breakfast, or you can leave if you've got to run.'

'Sure,' I smiled, sitting up in bed and patting my matted hair. 'I might be gone when you're done in the shower. I'll just check how long it takes to get home.'

As soon as I heard the rush of water, I stopped pretending to look at my phone and sidled out of his room and into the hallway, snatching my bag as I went. Standing in my sweaty dress and with scarecrow hair, only half an eyebrow still filled in, I glanced at my reflection in the mirror and thought, *fucking hell.* I looked terrible. It was kind of fun though, in a horrifying way. I'd never seen myself so bedraggled.

With a small smile, I made my way to the front door. Only it wasn't the front door, I realised, upon opening it and finding a man in his boxers, a bowl of cereal in his lap.

'Shit,' I said to the floor. 'Oh God. I'm sorry.'

After yanking the door closed, I cracked it open again.

'Which one's the front door?'

'Next one,' Matt's flatmate told me witheringly.

With a grateful nod, I blundered out of the dark flat and into the white morning light. Looking around, I remembered that I was in Haymarket — an area heaving with young suits on their morning commute. Conscious of the fact that I didn't blend into this crowd in my day-old clothes and messy hair, I made the humiliating yet exhilarating journey back to Old Town.

Because yes, there was something delicious about the embarrassment. Something thrilling about the fact that people would look at me and *see sex*. Here I was, a woman who had had sex last night, I thought with relish. Finally, I was part of the club.

A few moments before I reached my flat, I crossed paths with two actual nuns and decided that this was the most appalling walk-of-shame possible. I grinned, already messaging three different group chats.

———————◆———————

Gradually I felt my anxieties around sex melt away. Matt didn't just show me that I could have sex without shame; he also showed me that I could lie in bed with someone and feel safe. It really was a revelation – that intimacy could feel comforting, rather than compromising. That there was nothing inherently wrong or dirty about sex. And it's something I could enjoy, too, I discovered at the age of 24.

Finally free of my hang-ups at the end of 2018 (or so I thought), I decided to have a one-night stand with someone I'd met on a dating app. It was my first real foray into casual sex; the first time I loosened my grip on the pearls. And it was a slightly awkward, but kind of wonderful, experience.

I smiled broadly when I left his flat the next morning, convinced that I'd been wrong about sex for years. For so long I'd seen it as this dangerous, frightening thing, but I decided that the Bad Thing was a one-off. Nobody would ever make me feel that way again.

It was a deeply encouraging thought.

Thrillingly, I also discovered that I could find power in sex. Power and fun and self-actualisation. So I could live like a man if I wanted to, I concluded. From this day forward, I would have my cake and eat it.

When the conversation fizzled between the one-night stand and I, so did my obsession with 'not being that kind of girl'. If people called me a slut, who cared? I'd wear that word like a badge of honour. Yes, as 2019 opened before me, I decided to have as much sex as I wanted, and with whoever I wanted to have it with. All I needed was mutual attraction, a glass of wine, and my (now) lucky black dress.

I felt exhilarated; born again. I wasn't *Sex and the City*'s discerning, careful Charlotte anymore. I was liberated and fearless. I was Samantha.

CHAPTER 1

Joel

One thing you must never, ever do, is write on your dating profile that you are a model. Especially when your modelling credentials are tenuous, as they always are.

Not that this discouraged me. Joel was, in fairness, very modelesque. Athletic build, big, brown eyes, 100-megawatt smile. And if I was to be a connoisseur of casual sex in 2019, he fit the bill.

Joel was also the most promising man I'd encountered in what felt like years. I'd been dating in London for a couple of months now, having thrown myself into the dating pool, and for a while the waters were generally grim. One of my first Tinder dates was with a musician who, at first, seemed so appealing. He was a handsome, impressive Australian, who was studying at the Royal Academy of Music; pounding a piano in his black-and-white profile picture, a bouffant hanging over his eyes.

But he painted a very different picture when I saw him in person. Hunched in the corner of the pub we'd agreed on, Max was tense, diminutive, and pressed as closely to the wall as he could manage. He stuck out a hand when he saw me, the other arm still pinned to the wall. Shaking it, I smiled down at two saucer-like eyes almost overspilling with fear.

Mutually baffled by the formality of the handshake, we took each other in.

'Sorry I'm late,' I opened nervously, pulling my skirt down as I sat. 'Have you been waiting long?'

Max considered the question, staring out into the middle distance.

'No,' he answered at length.

'Oh. Okay, good,' I smiled.

Silence. Glancing from his blank expression to the menu between us, I tried to get a read on the date. Would this be unbearably painful, I wondered, or would Max's nerves thaw with a drink? Seizing the thought, I said: 'I'm going to the bar. Would you like anything?'

He nodded slowly, a strange, unreadable expression on his face.

'Yeah. Pint of Amstel, please.'

When I returned to the table, Max accepted the drink with another stoic nod, and silence returned. I shuffled awkwardly in my seat, asking him a question about his degree and what it was like at the Royal Academy of Music. He responded by staring past my shoulder for a full ten seconds, eventually replying with a handful of words, uttered in that same, lulling monotone. Our evening continued in this agonising vein for a long, long time.

An hour later, I crouched in a toilet cubicle downstairs and wondered how I'd make my escape. This wasn't like the movies, I realised. There were no windows to crawl through. I'd have to return with some sort of shaky excuse – an early morning, perhaps, or a bad stomach.

Approaching the table, I sheepishly opened my mouth just as he asked if I'd like another round.

'Oh! Thank you,' I replied, my stomach sinking. 'Maybe just a half pint, though. I've got an early morning tomorrow.'

'Sure,' Max nodded. He looked at me then with a small smile, his eyes expectant.

Baffled, I stared back at him.

'Oh ... did you – did you want me to grab it?'

He shook his head furiously.

'No, no. But maybe come with me so I get your order right?'

'Oh! Okay, sure.'

At the bar, Max ordered a half pint of Amstel for me and a full pint for him.

'£7, please,' the barmaid shouted over the music.

And suddenly, my date was staring at me. I turned my head to find two pleading eyes burning into mine.

'Would you mind?' he mouthed.

Heat crept up my neck and into my face. 'Sure,' I said, fumbling for my purse. Back at the table, I drank my half pint as quickly as I could. More questions came and went to pass the time, all directed at him. He didn't ask a single one in return.

And at long last, we parted at Camden station. Straining under the weight of this God-awful date, we promised to speak soon, but more or less ran to our respective modes of transport. I shook my head as I rushed through the tube barriers, wondering what on earth I'd just experienced. Wondering, also, if I could cope with dating in London.

It didn't get any better as December drew to a close. Tinder also introduced me to a beautiful Bavarian who tentatively kissed me outside a train station, sent me a picture of biscuits, added me as a friend on Facebook, and promptly fell off the face of the earth.

For God's sake, I thought. Were there no good men out there?

I wasn't alone in my dating despair. My friend Lydia had some cracking stories. We met to exchange them one day under the guise of shopping for books. With a grimace, she had just told me about a 'lovely, Teddy-bear-ish' guy who she met on Tinder and who had started 'frantically ripping at his dick' when he kissed her.

'It was like if he didn't do it, he'd drop down dead,' she said, a wall of warmth hitting us as we stepped into the bookshop. 'I ignored it for a bit, then we had sex.'

'Oh?' I asked, intrigued. 'And how was that?'

'Well, have you seen the episode of *Sex and the City* where they call a guy "The Jackrabbit"? The guy who gives Carrie a bad neck by pounding her into the next life?'

I nodded.

'It was just like that. I wanted to ask him: "Are *you* enjoying this? Really?" I certainly didn't cum.'

'Oh dear.'

Lydia paused as we entered the lift. 'I couldn't tell if he came that night,' she mused. Her face pinched, she looked as if she was trying to work out a crossword. 'I remember *hoping* he had, just so we could end it.'

'Oof. That bad?'

'That bad.'

Our conversation halted when the lift stopped and someone else stepped in. Two floors later, it resumed.

'So that was that?' I probed. 'He jackhammered you and then left the next morning?'

'If only it had been that simple!' Lydia cast her eyes to the ceiling. 'No. Sadly not. Eventually the sex fell by the wayside and we stopped. Then, the next morning, we had a chat and I asked him if he came last night.'

'And what did he say?'

'He said: "Not really, and, to be honest Lydia, it takes me a really, really long time to cum. Even when I'm wanking by myself, it takes me absolutely ages."'

'Ah.' I faltered as we stepped out of the lift, avoiding her gaze. Though I was curious, conversations like these put a magnifying glass on my lack of experience. I had no idea how common or uncommon it was for guys not to finish, and I didn't know what the appropriate response was. Was 'ah' an acceptable reply …?

Mercifully, Lydia didn't seem to notice. Looking around for the right section, she ploughed on with her story.

'So I was like: "Okay, fine, no worries." And he suggests we just wank next to each other, saying it would be really sexy.'

I raised my eyebrows. She nodded.

Searching for Hardy, Lydia lowered her voice as we began to scan the bookshelves.

'Well, I'm just like, it's not going to be very sexy watching you throw your dick to the other side of the room.'

'Right.'

'But we do it. The wanking next to each other. And all the time I'm looking at him in the corner of my eye, trying not to seem alarmed. It just looks so violent.'

'The dick ripping?'

'The rip-roaring dick-ripping. Neither of us came.'

Apologising between stifled laughter, I said: 'Sorry. That sounds awful.'

'It was … not great.'

'So how did you leave things?'

'Well, he texted me the next day.' A mutual grimace. 'And I just went back with some narrative of us "wanting different things", and "being in different places".'

'He wanted to rip his dick off and you didn't want to watch him do it?'

'In fewer words, yes.'

I nodded slowly, chuckling.

'A good excuse, that one. No one can argue with something as vague as "wanting different things" and being in "different places". What does it even mean?'

'Well, what else could I say?' Lydia asked, sounding slightly defensive. '"You had sex with me like you hadn't drunk in years and were drilling me for water?"'

She enjoyed my story about the stingy Australian, adding with glee: 'I see your Australian and raise you Someone Worse.'

I glanced up from an edition of *Tess* with a suspicious frown. 'No way.'

'Oh yeah. A few weeks ago I went for dinner with a guy and ordered a *salad* because the date was going so badly. He ordered a starter, a main, a dessert and three cocktails and asked if we could go halves.'

'No?' I winced.

'Yep. I had one drink.'

Our laughter came like air being let out of a balloon.

'Oh, what the fuck,' Lydia sighed afterwards. 'Bonnie Tyler was right: where *have* all the good men gone?'

Here's one! Here's one! I thought when I fell upon Joel's Tinder profile.

I happened upon it while walking around an art gallery with my university friend Beth, techno music pulsing in the background.

'Look at this guy,' I said, holding my phone up at Beth, who had been staring at *A Bigger Splash*.

'Oh.' Her eyebrows shot up. 'Yeah. He's nice. Very good-looking.'

'Right?'

Lowering onto a bench, Beth took my phone. Scrolling down his profile, she laughed.

'Have you seen that his hobbies include "fire breathing" and "Hungarian throat singing"?' she asked.

'Which is interesting,' I replied hopefully.

'Yeah.' She chuckled. 'Or insane.'

'Insane or, er, eccentric?'

'A thin line between those things.'

Standing, Beth handed my phone back with a wry smile. I went on staring down at Joel as we ambled through the gallery, almost falling down some stairs in the process. And then, with a jolt, I looked down to see that he'd messaged me.

Hey Kitty, Joel said. *Winky face.*

Winky face? Hm … I wasn't sure if I was turned off or intrigued. Maybe a bit of both.

Hello! I replied. No winky face. *Have you done much Hungarian throat singing lately?*

His response came just as fast.

Oh, yeah. That's a standard Tuesday night for me. I'll take you out sometime and show you how to do it.

Wow. That was forward, I thought, faltering. And also kind of weird. I'd been on some strange dates, but there was no way I was going to throat sing in the middle of a restaurant. Still … I remained intrigued. He seemed funny and *God*, so attractive. Was I actually going to go on a date with a model? A model with a sense of humour?

As our conversation developed, I grew more and more optimistic. Perhaps we didn't have that much in common, but he was hot and funny and that ticked every box I needed ticking at that time. Scrolling through his madcap messages, I chortled from the gallery's pink toilets as one quip followed the next. He made a more concrete proposition later on, asking if I wanted to meet on Friday. *Sure*, I replied, my heart pounding. Camden worked.

In all honesty, I wasn't sure if Camden did work. I'd lived in North London for a few months now, but in all that time hadn't quite worked Camden out.

If you're unfamiliar, let me paint you a picture. Walk down Camden High Street and you'll find crowds of tourists jostling over tat hanging from street stalls, musical history printed in bulk on £10 T-shirts. Look up at the houses and you'll see some flats in a crumbling state of disrepair, others worth millions. The nightlife is varied, too: from humble pubs with chipping paint to polished clubs like Blues Kitchen, or hole-in-the-wall bars like Spiritual. I started open-micing there (with varying success) when I began pursuing a singing career, and the only mainstay of that particular bar was a bearded brunette who apparently owned the place, and a smoky-eyed 25-year-old who worked at the local music shop. Besides those two, you could see anyone from the next Amy Winehouse to men who thought they were the next Bob Dylan, but who should have limited their singing to the shower. Whichever you got, it was a madly entertaining night.

This eccentricity echoed throughout the streets of Camden. One summer I went down to Camden Lock to spend a wholesome day riding a canal boat to Little Venice, and didn't even bother telling my friend that, prior to this, I'd seen a bloody-handed man stumbling around outside the underground and a clown shouting at me from the open window of his Fiat 500. Why would I bother? That was Camden for you.

Like the rest of London, it was a hodgepodge of rich and poor, gritty and contrived, which created a hazy, electric atmosphere. Looking down at Joel's message, I wasn't sure if it *was* the best place for a date, but couldn't think of an alternative.

We settled on the World's End, a pub which bottled Camden's scattiness. Like the TARDIS, it extends forever, with no end of dingy lighting and industrial chic in sight. Its clientele is varied – pierced, leather-clad teenagers hunching at the bar next to grubby old men and clean, city professionals. I elbowed my way up to the bar next to one of the latter and ordered a large glass of wine.

Settling on a bench downstairs, I sat with my wine and my wine alone for 30 minutes. Twenty minutes in, I realised that I'd never waited this long for a date. Restlessly, I crossed and uncrossed my legs, then recrossed them again. Maybe he'd got held up at work or on the train, but still, I couldn't believe it.

Getting antsy, I was looking at my blank phone screen and wondering if I should go home, when Joel appeared.

I drew a sharp intake of breath when he rounded the corner. Fucking hell, this was a *very* fine man. He was undeniably, radiantly, good-looking; a fresh-from-a-magazine kind of fit. The sort of handsome you'd see working in Hollister.

As it transpired, Joel was also two things that are good on a first date: energetic and enthusiastic. Approaching the table, he smiled down at me like I was something nice he'd fallen upon by accident – a pound coin wedged between two sofa cushions, or the last Malteser in a box you were about to throw away. And instead of sitting in the chair opposite, as the normal, slightly awkward first-date rules dictate, he plopped down on the bench beside me.

'Hey! How's it going? You look hot,' he announced.

'Oh. Heh.' I blinked him in, once again surprised at how forward he was. 'Thanks. You're not so bad yourself.'

I was quite proud of that, and sat back in my chair smiling. I'd not only managed to speak in full sentences, I'd also attempted something vaguely flirty. Maybe this date was going to be a success.

Joel smiled back, removing his jacket and dropping his rucksack on the floor. 'So, tell me about yourself, Kitty.'

I guffawed. 'God, we're going with that cliché are we?'

'Yes, I'm afraid so. Go on.' Here he brushed an errant curl from the side of my face, his brown eyes huge and inquisitive. 'I need to know how you're still single.'

I faltered, blinking at Joel again. 'Er, well I moved to London a few months ago and haven't been dating much, I suppose. You're one of the first Tinder dates I've had, actually.'

'Ah! And how were the other ones?'

'Terrible, for the most part.'

Joel laughed, running a finger loosely up and down my forearm. It was casual and vague but again very, very forward. 'And when was your last relationship?' he asked.

Almost spluttering, I looked up at Joel, wondering how often he did this with women he'd just met.

'What's with the twenty questions?'

'Well, this *is* a date, isn't it?' Joel grinned back. 'I'm just trying to get to know you, Kitty. Come on, you don't have anything to hide, do you?'

Closing my mouth, I tried to suppress the alarm bells ringing in my mind. The thing was, I *did* have things to hide. Things like: 'I've only recently lost my virginity' and 'I've never had a relationship'. Should I be honest and tell him that I'd never had a boyfriend? Would that put him off?

'Oh, it was years and years ago now,' I lied, looking down at the table.

'*Years?* Plural?' He paused. 'Interesting. So it's been a while?'

I nodded, my face burning.

'Okay. And when did you lose your virginity?'

I actually did choke on my wine this time. 'Are you kidding?' I asked with a nervous bout of laughter, wiping my mouth. 'Are you actually asking me when I lost my virginity five minutes into meeting me?'

'Yeah! Why wouldn't I?' Urgh. Joel had an insufferable way of making you just as enthusiastic as he was about something. I found myself smiling again in return. 'Like I said, I just want to get to know you.'

'Um. Well, alright,' I sighed. The alarm bells were sounding again. And just like before, I found myself lying. 'Eighteen,' I shrugged at him.

'Wow!' Joel sat back, taking me in anew. 'That's late.'

Smiling blankly, I wondered how he would have responded had I said '22'.

'What about you?'

'Fourteen.' The answer came quickly and confidently. Tilting his head back slightly, he watched my response with amusement.

'Well, I'd say that's a bit early, to be honest,' I blustered.

Joel shook his head as he laughed. 'It's really not. You *are* innocent, aren't you?' And with a flash of teeth, he began moving his hands up and down my thighs. 'I could tell as soon as I walked in.'

Maybe it was the glass of wine I'd nearly choked on, but that line didn't make me feel nearly as queasy as it should have done. And it didn't make me run for the hills, as it also should have done. If I was to *really* throw myself into dating and casual sex, I had to give people like Joel a chance, my tipsy brain told me. He seemed interested, which was exciting, and he was probably only in it for the sex, too, which was great. At this point, I didn't know what kind of sex I wanted, but I was excited to experiment. Everything was for the sake of experience during this time – I'd go home with a slightly leery stranger just to see what happened.

Needless to say, I was very naive about what *could* happen behind closed doors. I hadn't given much thought to what I would or wouldn't do in the bedroom; where I would draw a line and whether that line would be respected. As I drunk in Joel's dark eyes, sex was just a gleaming, enticing, slightly mysterious prospect. It made me nervous, but it didn't make me afraid. I didn't know enough about casual sex to feel afraid yet.

What I did know was that I wanted to try it out. I wasn't ready for a relationship, having only just stepped onto the dating scene and got over my hesitancies around sex. I was so late to the game, it seemed premature to take myself out of it. So casual sex it was, à la Samantha Jones. And Samantha would definitely go home with someone like Joel.

We didn't speak for much longer. A few minutes later, I was answering another of Joel's quickfire questions when he launched his tongue into my mouth. There was nothing hesitant about his kiss – it was deep and kind of rough, one hand sliding under the back of my tights.

We were a nauseating sight. Another two glasses in and I'd relocated my arse into his lap while he fumbled around my hosiery like he was looking for a pair of keys. I felt hot and bothered and thrilled and thrown off, all at the same time.

Unsurprisingly, the prospect of 'your place or mine' soon cropped up. He whispered it into my neck while I watched the January snow fall outside, considering how romantic and unromantic the scene felt. A romantic-comedy-porno-hybrid.

'Not tonight,' I whispered back, my heart rattling. Because yes, I was up for casual sex, but did I want to do it on the first date? Would that make me too much of a slut? After all, didn't they change the first episode of *Friends* so that Monica didn't have sex with a guy on a first date because NBC thought it made her a little too slaggy? *EastEnders'* Kat Slater's words began to echo around my head: 'I didn't become a *little* bit of a slag. I became a TOTAL SLAG.' Was I ready to go full Kat Slater? Hm, probably not.

And certainly not tonight, I decided. Joel didn't accept defeat lightly, however, vigorously kissing me under his umbrella at the traffic lights after we left the pub, and then up against a wall in Camden station. While his tongue was in my mouth, a bald, middle-aged man noted with disgust: 'People out here are acting like they're in *High School Musical.*' And I'm still unsure of what to make of that.

As we parted, Joel told me that this had been a very good first date. Tittering, I agreed, then peeled myself away and stumbled tipsily through the barriers.

I giggled like a loser all the way home.

For our second date, Joel and I chose the Little Bat in Highbury and Islington. Unlike the World's End, it's a swish bar with a bathroom I would happily live in. Pushing open the toilet door, I looked up to see vines snaking down from the ceiling, classical music echoing around the chamber-like walls. When I stepped into a cubicle, I noticed there was even a cabinet complete with q-tips to fix your makeup.

I dipped a couple of these into my makeup remover to fix my eyeliner, trying to ignore my panicked expression in the mirror. Yes, I'd brought makeup remover with me. *No*, that didn't mean anything was going to happen tonight. But I wanted to be prepared in case it did …

The question was: was I ready to have sex again? It had been two months since my first one-night stand with a stranger, and I'd been foaming at the mouth to climb into bed with someone else. Still, with the prospect really on the horizon, I paled under the pressure. He was a sexually charged model; I was barely sexually active. What would he expect in the bedroom, and would I be able to deliver?

Feeling scattered, I returned to Joel, who was languishing on a velvet sofa. He smiled at me crookedly, one arm draped over the back of the seat, the top button of his shirt loose. Bloody hell. It was like walking into a Hugo Boss ad.

'Hello,' I squeaked.

'Hello,' Joel returned coolly. 'It's lovely to see you again.' Leaning forward, he kissed me on the cheek.

And that was where the gentility ended. Our second date followed the same pattern as our first, but with even less conversation and even more tongue. At one point I felt his hand slide down the back of my underwear, getting lost in synthetic lace.

Classy as it was, the Little Bat didn't look kindly on mine and Joel's corner sofa canoodling. When the waiter brought the bill over and I complimented the wine, he glared at me with disdain. 'Yes,' he said curtly. 'I could certainly see that you were *enjoying yourself.*'

I drew my lips together, blinking.

Joel and I laughed conspiratorially when he wheeled away. 'He'll be glad to see the back of us,' I said quietly.

'Yeah.' Joel chuckled. 'Do you want to go to Wetherspoons? It's around the corner, and maybe more our scene.'

'God, that can't be good,' I muttered. Nonetheless, I nodded.

After half an hour in the Highbury and Islington Wetherspoons (one of the inferior ones, both sticky and weird), we made the journey back to Joel's house.

Comfortably tipsy, I felt my nerves fall away. This was going to be fun, I thought, clinging onto his firm body as we waited for the Uber. Suddenly, I felt safe. Excited. Ready and raring to have sex again. *And with a model, too!* an inner voice gloated. This was one for the bucket list.

Joel became slightly more withdrawn on the drive to his flat. He gave me a gentle smile in the dark, gingerly placing his hand on top of mine, and was perfectly mute in the lift up to his floor. Something appeared to have happened in the time it took to get from Highbury and Islington to Finsbury Park. I hoped this silence stemmed from comfort rather than a sudden lack of confidence, wondering with a twinge of worry if he'd turn into Matt. Would he lie rigidly next to me, fully clothed, and then pounce on me in the dark? Would I have to watch *Anchorman 2* again? Surely not.

These thoughts stopped abruptly when I stepped into his bedroom. All of a sudden, I was far more preoccupied with how much *stuff* there was around us. Towers upon towers of unde-termined *things*, and barely any of the brown, carpeted floor space uncovered. It was so dank and small and full, I observed, and yet Joel was so lean and sparkly and vibrant. Strange. I'd imagined his flat to be all chrome or something.

When the initial shock had passed, I sat down on the bed and smiled up at him. With his own soft smile, Joel pushed me down so that he could loom over me. Ah, the confidence was definitely back! I registered with relief. Good. This wasn't going to be weird.

And for a couple of minutes, it wasn't. We kissed deeply, passionately; his hands circling my thighs, mine undoing his shirt buttons. Then Joel began to reach for something beside the bed.

I couldn't tell what it was at first, but in my peripheral vision I saw him bringing something up, twisting it around his hand. It was long and black, I noted. Then he wound it around my wrist and tightened it.

Before I had time to register what was going on, I saw that my right wrist was now pinned above my head. What the ...? He pulled the left one into another black restraint, and then up that one went as well, the whole thing connected by some kind of pulley system. Both my ankles followed suit – a limb to each post.

I looked up at Joel and laughed in pure, manic shock. He smiled mischievously back at me.

'You know, you can say "no" at any time,' he purred, bending down to kiss my legs.

Um! Okay? So here it was. *This* was now happening, apparently. I'd barely lost my virginity and I was being tied up in a stranger's bedroom. Looking back, I wonder why I didn't panic at that moment. Why I didn't pull at my restraints or ask to be set free. Yes, I was ready for casual, even experimental sex, but this was a little extreme. For all I knew, he could have been an axe murderer or a ... furry, or something.

At the time, however, I remember it being a little like that episode in *Father Ted* – the one where he thinks that he'll have a meltdown if anything happens to the plane, but then when it actually does, this air of calm falls over him. What will be will be, I told myself vaguely, looking at my trussed-up ankles. If I'm found dead tied to a bed in North London, *que sera sera*. Etc.

Fortunately, Joel didn't stab me or pull out a pair of ears and a tail, but he did proceed to produce a large, drawstring sack.

I watched him root around inside it, smiling in a rehearsed, self-assured way. And then, like a raunchy Father Christmas, he pulled out a purple, pebble-shaped thing which started to vibrate in his hand. I was no stranger to vibrators, but had never seen one like *that*.

He looked at me intently as he held it against me. I gasped. Okay, so this was – this was great. My inability to move made the pleasure intoxicating, almost unbearable. Holy shit, I was actually going to have an orgasm, I realised. Right here in front of him.

Next came an enormous dildo (also purple), and finally an unwieldy white device which he needed to plug into the wall. Joel struggled with its tangled lead for a painful few seconds, then reached over my body and grappled to plug it into a socket.

I've since discovered that this Unidentified Plug-in Object is called a Magic Wand, and, quite honestly? My soul left my body. I felt myself float up out of my physical form and watched myself being annihilated by what looked like a comically large microphone down below. Fucking *hell*. I felt disconcerted and serene all at the same time.

When the sack had returned to its place under the bed, Joel began to untie me. Free at last, I held my wrists and watched him surreptitiously lay two towels on the mattress. Then he looked up at me and said the worst words I've ever heard.

'Well, you look like a squirter,' he smirked.

You. Look. Like. A. Squirter.

I turned my head, opening my mouth to ask the first of many questions I'd never verbalise. How did someone *look* like a squirter? I wanted to ask. More pressingly (if egotistically), how did *I* look like a squirter? Could people tell when they saw me in the street? Did they squint at me for a moment and then nod, thinking: 'Ah yes, another squirter'?

Did we squirters walk around with big red 'S's pinned to our chests?

I put my chagrin aside as Joel pulled himself into me. Lord, he had an enormous cock. We tried three positions in total and I came twice.

Squirter or not, I had conquered sex at last.

———

Sleeping next to Joel was uncomfortable. He promptly fell asleep after we had sex, rolling over to leave me on the cold side of the mattress. Gazing at my empty restraints hanging limply from the bed frame, I considered how acutely untouched I suddenly felt. I needed his warm arms around me, telling me that – though we were strangers – we'd just done something intimate and hot-blooded and human. Instead, I felt like a glorified sock.

Open-eyed and peeved, I continued to lie there, stiffly, until he finally made some attempt at cuddling me. This translated to him lazily stretching a leg over mine, one arm plonked over my side so that it dangled over the edge of the bed. And bloody hell, it weighed a tonne. I went from being very cold to very,

very hot, pinned to this grubby mattress in a small room from *Hoarder's Anonymous*, eager for the dulcet tones of my alarm clock to set me free.

At the first peal a few hours later, I wriggled out from under Joel's arm and dove into my clothes.

'Oh, are you going?' he croaked from the bed.

'Yeah, sorry.' I looked back at him briefly, and saw that his eyes were still closed.

'Work?'

'Yeah. I start at nine.'

'Cool, well …' Rubbing his eyes, Joel turned over. 'I'll message you,' he told the wall.

I nodded, taking my bag from the floor.

After fumbling my way through a maze of corridors and walkways, I finally found the lift and pressed Ground Floor, glancing at my dishevelled reflection in the mirror. Oof, it was even worse than the morning after Matt. I looked like I'd been shagged through a hedge backwards.

Stepping out of the tower block, I lifted my face to the white sky and let the raindrops find me. The rain continued falling in a light, morning drizzle as I ambled about, searching for Finsbury Park station. When I finally found it, I called Beth and cackled down the phone.

'He did *what*?' she near-shouted.

'I know.' Snickering, I plugged the other ear as the 'whoosh' of a train went by.

'And he had a sack?'

'He had a *sack*.'

Beth paused. I felt that she might be shaking her head. 'From this day on, we will only refer to him as Sex Santa,' she said.

'Okay. Sounds about right.'

A little after nine and slightly less dishevelled, I joined my colleagues Layla and Aisling in the lift up to our office.

'Good date?' Layla asked as I winced at the mirror.

'*Mad* date.' I tried to tuck a matted curl behind my ear, sighing.

She laughed. 'You sound shell-shocked.'

'I am a bit. He, er ...' Pausing, I glanced at the woman who was also my boss. My hesitation was brief, however; the startup we both worked for was hardly known for its professionalism. Like so many startups before it, the office was brimming with beanbags, faulty coffee machines and offbeat characters who were far too honest about their lifestyles. The Head of Design, for instance, was a stringy, middle-aged man who wore the exact same outfit everyday, his rings and bangles jangling as he swaggered over to the water cooler. Rumour had it that he'd directed porn before he joined the company.

Glancing back at my reflection, I continued: 'Well, I won't say what he did exactly but ... wow.'

'Oh, man. I'm jealous.'

'Wait. Was this that Joel guy?' Aisling asked me, her eyes narrowing.

I nodded.

Something seemed to pass over her face, as if she'd half-remembered a conversation she once had. Nonetheless, she didn't say anything else.

That changed a few days later, when Aisling showed me a picture of Joel on her phone and asked if it was him. It was on her kink-friendly hook-up app, Feeld, and his name on the platform was 'Gerp'. Reading Gerp's bio, I realised that the Magic Wand was just the tip of the iceberg.

'What's this Japanese rope thing?' I hissed, my eyes popping out of my head.

Aisling searched for it on Wikipedia, pounding her keyboard. Agog, we twisted our necks to take in the illustration at the top of the page.

'Well bloody hell, I'm not doing *that*,' I muttered. Aisling laughed.

To my surprise, Gerp/Joel did message that day, but the message was a little lacklustre. I wondered if he really had any intention of seeing me again, but didn't give myself the opportunity to find out – I left his text unanswered. I'd never ghosted anyone before, and did feel a little guilty, but how did you tell someone you'd met twice that you didn't want to be tied to their ceiling? I didn't want to be trussed up like a hunk of meat in a butcher's window, slowly rotating and wondering how I'd got there.

No shame if you're into that sort of thing, of course. But it was a bit much for me.

'Bloody hell,' I sighed, closing my eyes that evening as I leaned against the bus window. My dalliance into casual sex had got off to a slightly extreme start. But surely they wouldn't all be like that, I thought tentatively. Men, that is. Perhaps the next one would be a little more mellow.

———

Recently I told a new friend about Joel, and she wondered how I felt about him now.

It's tricky. I never felt exploited by him or coerced in any way, but, ruminating on it, it's interesting to look back on how accepting I was of being tied to a bed on the second date. Of a stranger winding ties around my wrists and ankles and only *then* telling me that I could say no. What if I hadn't felt able to say no at that point, incapacitated as I was?

Women are often led to believe that sex is something which might take us by surprise. Something flattering which we should go along with, in whatever form it takes. In *The Breakfast Club*, Bender sticks his head between Claire's legs and she slaps him, but guess what? She still ends up with him at the end of the film. It's a pattern we often see in movies, books and in real life: a woman is alarmed (maybe even horrified) by the sexual act of a man, but this shock eventually dissolves into quiet submission. Sex is something which is done *to* us, according to our sexist ideals of passive femininity. So take it as a compliment; go along for the ride.

I didn't give this much thought at the time. My night with Joel didn't feel compromising, it felt fun and lighthearted and sexy. Still, my silent submission was a precursor for what was to come.

CHAPTER 2

Jack

I met Jack two months after Joel.

I'd been on a short string of lacklustre dates during that time. The night before, I'd gone out with a spindly man with long, ring-bearing fingers and black shadows under his eyes. It quickly became apparent that Dracula and I had nothing in common, and he ended the ordeal by saying that he needed to visit his dog in hospital.

Dejected, I opened my Tinder the next morning to see that a six-foot-three man named Jack had 'Super Liked' me. Usually, this was a desperate plea to be avoided at all costs. But he had blonde waves, blue eyes, a wonky nose and smile. I was intrigued. After a thoughtful few moments, I matched.

Hello, Kitty, Jack's first message began. *You're very beautiful. What do you think about watching TV, getting high and eating fried chicken?*

I would like to point out that Jack was 32. And that I replied.

Thankfully, his conversation improved. As we volleyed, I realised that Jack was not only good-looking; he was also interesting, funny and smart. He was doing a Science PhD, liked prison documentaries, and hadn't been on a good date in months. Hoping to turn his luck around, he asked if I wanted to meet him for a drink in Kentish Town. *Sure*, I said. *I'll meet you there after work.*

Shuffling into the office toilets, I found a dry patch beside the sink for my bag and began to apply lipstick. I'd gone for a nude: not too try-hard, and safe from travelling across my face after the first sip of wine. It was deliciously buttery, too.

Rubbing my lips together, I wondered if I'd kiss Jack tonight, and whether he'd taste like KFC. Oh Lord, I thought, buttoning my bag. What was I doing?

Humming with nerves, I slung it over my shoulder and pottered down to the Bull and Gate. I'd chosen this pub because it was a twenty-minute walk from my house, meaning I could quickly escape if he was as weird as his first message.

When I saw Jack at the bar, however, my mood quickly shifted. He was even more handsome in person. All strong arms, blue flannel and a worn leather jacket. I swooned a little more when he opened his mouth to reveal a soft, Northern Irish brogue.

'Kitty! So wonderful to meet you,' he greeted me, pulling me in for a hug.

Smiling into the warmth of his sturdy arms and creased jacket, I thought about how nice this was – this politeness and enthusiasm. After so many dates of drudgery and disappointment, it was exactly what I needed.

We took our beers to a bench by the window, looking at each other with a mutual, newfound hope. His hands flat on the table, Jack spoke about his job and I spoke about mine. Everything was thrilling to him, his blue eyes widening with every detail.

'I can't believe you sing,' he exclaimed at one point, reaching across the table for one of my hands. 'You should have put that on your profile. I would have super-liked you twice.'

I laughed down at our hands, shrugging. 'Yeah, well. It might not go anywhere. It probably won't.'

'No, it will.' Jack shook his head, his eyes intense. 'I have a feeling.'

Glancing up at him, I smiled, suddenly gooey. A lovely feeling of safety and affirmation crept into my chest, warming it through.

'Well, maybe ...' I paused, turning my glass in my hand. 'So, what are your hobbies?'

'Oh, nothing as interesting as that. I do a bit of drawing, but I'm not very good. Here,' he said, reaching for his phone. 'This is one I did a week ago.'

'Ah!' My eyes widened. 'And that's a ... that's a woman there?'

'That's a woman,' he confirmed. 'What do you think?'

'It's great.' Oh dear, I wasn't being very convincing. 'Although she has a very long arm.'

'That's not an arm, it's a leg,' Jack laughed. I joined him nervously, grateful he hadn't taken offence.

He insisted on buying the next round, and we remained in our window seat for hours. Three drinks in, Jack finally rounded the table and planted himself next to me, our fingers interlaced. He leaned down to kiss me then, and my head spun.

Jack's lips were delicate, and his kiss – tender one moment, urgent and hungry the next – completely floored me.

'Wow,' he breathed when we parted, his blue eyes bright. Happy and self-conscious, I laughed.

'Shall we get the bill?' I asked after a beat, keen to end the night on this glorious note. Jack nodded.

On the way to the station, he took hold of my shoulders, stopping me while we waited for the traffic lights to change.

'I would fucking love to see you again,' he told me, looking down with intense, almost desperate longing. I smiled again, impressed with how he wore his heart on his sleeve – how he didn't downplay his interest for the sake of seeming cool and aloof. Maybe this is what men in their thirties are like, I thought, full of optimism.

'I'd like that, too,' I enthused. 'Are you free next Friday?'

'I am.' Jack gave my shoulders a quick squeeze. 'I can't believe I'm going to have to wait that long, but next Friday it is.'

He kissed me again, and, as we parted, the green man appeared.

'Look at that!' he shouted as he crossed the road. 'What are the chances?'

I was smiling ear to ear as I walked home from the station. Jack's dating bio told me that he was only in London for the next month, but I was very happy to spend my April with him. I enjoyed how he made me feel: warm and secure and admired and appreciated. It was a nice change and a rare feeling in a pretty brutal dating landscape. I felt that I should hold onto it.

And if I accidentally fell in love with him, well, I could at least wave a hanky at the airport and cry on the train home.

Our second date was going swimmingly. Jack and I wandered around Chinatown, had dinner, and settled afterwards in a cosy pub with dark-green wallpaper. When we were thrown out at closing time, we relocated to a small, underground bar.

Before turning the corner to said bar, Jack told me that he'd been thinking a lot about our last kiss. I asked him if he wanted to recreate it (smooth! Who was this girl?), and leaned up on my tiptoes to neck him in the street. God, it was even better than the first time.

We were giddy walking downstairs, pushing through a beaded curtain to reveal a hot, narrow room. A man with a corduroy jacket and book glanced up at us, annoyed that we'd disturbed him. Meanwhile, a group of floppy-haired friends had congregated at the bar, ordering purple drinks and talking to the barman, who looked back at them with a vacant expression.

I sat with Jack at a table near said bar, our faces lit pink by a neon light overhead.

'This is cool,' I noted.

'Fun, isn't it? I wish I'd discovered this place years ago. Now, what would you like?'

'Ooh. I wouldn't mind a margarita.'

'Great. Two margaritas coming up.'

Our giddiness was exacerbated by the cocktails. Before long, Jack's hand had found my knee, then my thigh. We looked at each other carefully, quiet for a few moments. All of a sudden, I felt nervous.

'You have very beautiful eyes,' he said eventually, studying them. I felt my knees weaken, all of my limbs loosen. His own eyes were so intensely blue, and there was a brilliant, almost unbearable tension bubbling between us.

God. I'm not sure how much longer I can take this, I thought after a few moments.

By midnight, it became obvious that we'd be going home together. Without a word, we picked up our coats and walked to the tube hand in hand, blinking in its white light.

'It's half an hour to get to mine,' Jack told me, squinting a little. Silently, I nodded.

It was only when we were in the tunnels that I really considered what was about to happen. I let it sink in as we searched for the Victoria Line, my blood buzzing. I was nervous, but if sex with Jack was anything like kissing him, I was in for a good time. Fiddling with my bra strap, I looked at the back of his blonde head and repeated to myself: *We're going to have sex. We're going to have sex.*

Which was all very exciting until I sat down on the tube with him. When the train shifted, I began to find Jack difficult to decipher. He seemed nervous suddenly; scatty, rather than exuberant. At one turn he was gentlemanly and respectful: 'We don't have to do anything when we get back to mine, you know.' At the next, he was verging on creepy: 'I know women and feminists don't like it when drivers honk their horn at girls, but if I saw you in the street I would *honk* my fucking *horn.*'

This latter comment surprised me. I said nothing in response, awkwardly laughing and deciding to ignore it. Focusing instead on the ads above the opposite seats, I thought: 'This is fine. It's just pre-sex nerves. He's bad at flirting, which isn't a big deal. And hey, we all say weird things when we're nervous.' Examining the marketing spiel for a bottle of iron supplements, I assured myself I could push his peculiarities under the rug.

All the same, I was relieved when we climbed the steps to the street. Lifting my face to the cool air, I glanced over at Jack, who seemed a little more calm. Perhaps it was the open space or the fresh air, but his shoulders started to sag.

'Right, let's stop on the way back for a bottle of wine,' he smiled down at me, pulling me under his arm.

'Sure,' I acquiesced, hoping that it wouldn't stain my teeth.

I nearly dropped the bottle when we arrived at his, staring open-mouthed at the horizon.

'You can see the Shard?' I baulked. 'The Shard? From your front door?'

Staring at him, I tried not to look as incredulous as I very much was. Wasn't this guy a student?

'Yeah,' Jack chuckled. 'It's alright, isn't it?'

I blinked at him in awe. It was more than alright. Jack's flat was the sort of place I'd imagined Joel living in. Spacious and modern with floor-to-ceiling windows, it even had a balcony.

We sat out there to smoke a spliff for a while and talk about nothing. With each drag, Jack became visibly more relaxed, while I felt unchanged. This might be because I was doing it wrong and he couldn't be bothered to correct me, but I was relieved, whatever the reason. I'd only toyed with weed twice in my life. The first time I witnessed a friend singe part of her fringe off, and was too high to respond at anything other than a snail's pace (which isn't ideal when smoke is emanating from your friend's head). Later that day I attempted to go home but had to return to hers five minutes later, raving over text about 'being too high for this' and 'all the houses looking the same'.

The second time was in Amsterdam. Pumped up with the kind of glee only a tourist in the Netherlands knows, I went to a café and ate an entire space cake, chasing this with half a spliff. Staring forlornly at a spaced-out couple by the door, I complained to my friend Tim that I felt nothing. Then all of a sudden I felt everything, all at once. Face-down on the table, I groaned loudly, tumbling down through different dimensions.

'I can't find the right one,' I moaned into the woodwork.

'Well, you're really representing the British well here,' I heard Tim say from somewhere up above. Minutes later he ferried me home, my face gaunt and slightly yellow.

Not wanting to lie beside Jack's toilet all night mumbling about the passage of time, I passed the spliff back to him and said I'd had enough.

An hour later and sobered up (we'd forgotten about the wine), I followed Jack into his bedroom. As he shut the door, I glanced around, suddenly speechless.

Jack's room was ... well, it was not in line with the rest of the flat's sophistication, that's for sure. Translated into physical objects, his adolescent-like enthusiasm for fried chicken, getting high and my totally-rad hotness seemed exactly that: adolescent-like. A wooden dragon puffed out incense in the corner. Empty cans of fizz littered the desk. The bin was overflowing and posters flanked us on either side, their corners making a break for freedom. And, in spite of the dragon's best efforts, the room smelled a little stale.

Oh God. Was I in the room of a 32-year-old man or a sixteen-year-old boy? Oh no, I thought for the fifth time in ten seconds. This was not good. Regret started to hit me with the force of a tidal wave.

And then all of a sudden I felt hands slide around my waist, a pair of lips in the crook of my neck. Soon enough, my reservations began to melt. Jack buried his face in my hair, his hot breath on the side of my face. As he pulled me down onto the bed beside him, his tongue deep in my mouth, I let out a small moan.

You know what? He's good at this, I assured myself. He's a good kisser and a 32-year-old man, who was probably so busy studying rocket science that he didn't have time to clean. And that Irish accent could make up for anything, right?

Well, not quite. As good as he was at kissing, I was alarmed to see that Jack became a different person with sex. The more we got into it, the stranger he became. As we undressed he became as impassioned as a street preacher; as frantic as a bitch in heat. I wondered if he'd break out of my embrace to go and howl at the moon at one point.

'I want *to eat you*,' he gasped, clawing off my top and sinking his nails into my skin.

Unsure of how to respond, I said nothing, moving to pull my skirt down. But Jack placed a hand on mine, stopping me.

'No,' he pleaded. 'Keep it on.'

I glanced at him with misgiving, removing my hands. 'Alright,' I shrugged. It felt a little odd to be completely nude bar a clingy pencil skirt, but whatever.

Once he was inside me, Jack whispered in my ear: 'It's because I have this fantasy [thrust] ... this fantasy that we're on the dance-floor [thrust-thrust] ... and that I'm [tugging on my skirt] protecting your dignity.'

I swallowed a burst of laughter, trying to concentrate on the ceiling. My dignity would have been out of the window, I wanted to tell him. With two other things giving me away, the skirt wouldn't have done much good.

God. If you're going to bring a fantasy into the bedroom, at least make it vaguely believable.

Plus, I now had Sophie Ellis-Bextor's 'Murder on the Dancefloor' in my head. And no one wants to be screwed to that song, believe me.

In spite of all of the above, Jack's rapture and animalistic adrenaline did eventually make for some fun sex. He had an amazing physique and strong, firm arms, tossing me around with an open mouth, curls coiling in the heat. It was even better than my dalliance with the Magic Wand, in the end.

Drinking in his adulation, I climbed on top of Jack at one point and screwed him hard, gently pushing his chest down when he rose to kiss me. He grinned under my hands, fingers splayed, and I smiled back. I'd never known a power like this.

Moments later we came in perfect synchrony and fell down next to each other, huffing and puffing and sweating and smiling.

'Fuck me. That was great,' Jack panted, running his hands over his face.

I felt like I was floating, and tucked myself under his arm happily, pulling my body as close to his as I possibly could.

'It was,' I sighed.

Jack squeezed my shoulder in response, and then ruined the moment with the most peculiar sentence yet.

'So, Kitty, I was wondering,' he began, 'would you like to join my religion?'

My smile dropped. His what? I turned my face to stare up at Jack, its colour draining.

'Your what?'

'You know, my religion,' he said plainly. 'I've mentioned it a couple of times before.'

I continued staring at Jack, trying my best to absorb this bombshell. Had he mentioned a religion before? *His* religion? Combing through my memories, I realised with horror that he had. But I'd thought he was joking! Who had their own religion? Apart from, you know, cultists?

'Oh, right. Yeah.' I fumbled around, grasping for something to say. What *was* his religion, and why was he bringing it up now? 'Um …'

'It's really just got some very basic, core values at its heart,' Jack quickly interjected, rubbing my arm. 'You know, just about how we should give up on things like other religions and science and society. How we should all just love each other and do nothing to harm anyone else.'

'Right, yes,' I said vaguely. 'That does sound nice.'

Registering the intensity in his face, I realised that diplomacy wasn't going to cut it.

'Um, yeah, sure,' I said, swallowing. Oh my God, had I just agreed to join a cult? Was this how it happened? They had you revelling in the ecstasy of sex one moment, then taking a blood oath the next? I eyed his bedroom window warily. Any mention of blood and I could probably climb out of there.

I desperately hoped that the lunacy would end there and that I could slip out the next morning. All I had to do was wait until it was light enough to get my things and go, I told myself in the darkness. I knew that sleep would make the time go faster, and willed my mind to stop racing.

But just as I was dozing off, Jack wedged a thumb inside my vagina and whispered: 'I have another fantasy.'

Oh no.

'So in this fantasy,' he said, 'you live in my house. Not this one – a big apartment at the top of a skyscraper with lots of rooms.'

'Mm. Sounds nice.'

'And you never leave. I keep you locked in there.'

Right.

'And you have all these little outfits that you wear only for me. Ones that I see and think: "Oh, she's done that on purpose."'

I closed my eyes and began breathing heavily, pretending to be asleep. I have to get out of here, I thought. I just had to get out.

Unfortunately, my escape the next morning was not easy. Jack was clingy, trapping me in his long arms and legs and kissing my neck. At the earliest possible moment I told him that I needed to catch a bus to visit my mum (which was true, but not for a few hours), and was alarmed when he asked if he could come, too.

'No,' I laughed, almost choking in the process.

Jack grabbed my waist and pulled me back into bed, yanking the duvet over us.

'Come on, don't go,' he murmured into my neck. 'I'll barricade the flat so you can't leave.'

'Er.' I hoped he was joking.

'Just *stay*. Come on, only for a couple of hours.'

'Can't,' I protested, wriggling free. 'I've got to catch this bus. Sorry.'

Finally, I broke out into the morning sunshine, and called Beth on the way to the station.

'Hello, how are you? I think I might have joined a cult last night,' I said, checking Citymapper.

'What?' she half-burbled, half-laughed.

'So I'm assuming that's never happened to you? I'm assuming that isn't just normal London dating stuff?'

'Well, no. It's, er ... it's never happened to me.'

'Alright.' I sighed. 'I've just left his and I'm getting on the tube and I'm pretty sure I still have cum in my hair. I didn't stick around for a shower ... is that bad?'

'Yes. Filth!' Beth laughed proudly. 'Will you see him again?'

'Absolutely not.'

I was still reeling from the night's events on my walk home from the tube, the spring sunshine strangely unsettling. How had there been such a complete 180 in the course of one night, I wondered. Jack had made me feel so safe and secure on that first date, then so confused and creeped out the next. How had I got him so wrong?

'Oh well,' I sighed again, wishing the birds would pipe down. It was a good story to bring to a party, and our fling had only ever been casual. There were no strings attached, and there was no pressure to meet him again. We'd both got what we wanted out of the affair, and that would hopefully be the last I'd hear from him.

My stomach dropped when he messaged, later that day.

Hey, Kitty, he said. *I had such a great time last night. Hope you have fun today.* xx

I stared at the message from the top deck of the megabus, my guts churning. I couldn't keep seeing this man after he'd invited me to join his religion, could I? I couldn't keep seeing him after he'd shared a fantasy about locking me away?

But surely I couldn't ghost him, either? Not after I'd ghosted Joel …

Eventually, I resolved to send short, blunt messages. Not unkind, but not enthusiastic either. Hopefully he'd get the message.

He did not. Two days later, Jack asked me out again.

'You don't have to go,' my flatmate Jen reminded me from the foot of our house's stairs.

'Yes, I do,' I wailed down from the top.

'But why?'

'Because he's bought two tickets for us to go and see a band. He's already *bought* them.'

I could hear her laughing from below.

'What band?' she asked, pulling her shoes on.

'A heavy metal band.'

'A WHAT?'

'A *heavy metal band.*'

Her laughter rose an octave. I grimaced. Well, this was a nightmare. Honestly, what had I got myself into?

Pulling on a simple black dress for our third date (not my lucky one, I wouldn't put that dress through tonight), I gave myself a pep talk in the mirror.

'Go in, stay for two hours, get out,' I muttered. It was a simple but effective plan. Hopefully there wouldn't be any talk of ceremonies or initiations or … whatever cults involved. Sighing, I grabbed my keys and headed to the station.

It was an uncharacteristically hot day for April. Stepping into Camden Town, the air felt muggy, the atmosphere fraught. Searching the crowds, my eyes fell on Jack but I almost didn't recognise him. Far from the clean, suave man in the cracked leather jacket, he looked as unwashed and unkempt as his bedroom, dark shadows under his eyes. Another tsunami of regret hit me. I wondered what tonight had in store, and why I'd even come in the first place.

Smiling vaguely, Jack greeted me with a kiss that felt distracted.

'You okay?' I asked, looking up at him.

He nodded, his mouth a thin line.

'Yeah, fine,' he replied. 'I didn't sleep too well, I suppose …'

Oh man. I wanted to roll my eyes. Apparently *he* didn't want to be here either, so what were we doing? Why had he asked me out? Well, it was too late to go back now – we were already here. So I pushed past my irritation and stepped with him into the venue, looking around at the ticket-holders.

There was more black leather and studs than you could shake a stick at, I observed, and one man had an actual mohawk. With a smile, I decided to forget about Jack and take in my first heavy metal gig.

To my surprise, I thoroughly enjoyed the experience. The gig was high-energy and fun – teenagers lobbing one another into the hot, wobbly air to crowd-surf. I didn't even mind the music, reverberating around the grimy walls and low ceiling. The only downer was Jack's mood, which was increasingly difficult to ignore. He was a million miles away, standing behind me with his arms glued to his sides. 'Is the band okay? I didn't think you'd like it,' he kept shouting into my ear.

'Yeah, it's great,' I grinned each time, looking back at him. His own expression didn't move.

All in all, he seemed jittery. Self-conscious. Unsure of himself and uneasy in his own skin. For some reason, he was even more scattered than he'd been on the tube over to his place, so I was surprised when he asked if I wanted to grab a drink as the band packed up.

'Oh. Okay, sure,' I replied, looking up at Jack hesitantly. Damn it, why hadn't I thought of an excuse? And why did he want to extend the date when he was clearly having an awful time?

'Let's go to the World's End,' he said, nodding. 'It's just a couple doors down from here.' Not that place again, I thought, but agreed. We'd have one drink, then leave.

Jostling our way to the bar, Jack and I laughed with the man next to us, until Jack dragged the joke on for so long that the stranger, now uncomfortable, just upped and walked away. My guts twisted again as I looked up at him. Why am I here with this strange man? I wondered, watching Jack's now stony expression.

'Are you okay?' I asked him again as we sat down with our drinks.

'Fine,' he said testily, then launched into a 30-minute rant as if I was taking notes for an autobiography, talking about everyone who had ever wronged him – his parents, his sister, the friend he'd recently fought with – and 'why I get every job I interview for, because people love me'.

I blinked at this last statement. 'Well, that's good?'

'No, it's not,' he retorted. 'I don't have a job *now*. That's why I'm moving back to Ireland, with my parents. I just couldn't stand the bullshit.' He fell silent, considering his beer glass with misery in his eyes.

Right. So was this a date or a therapy session? I wasn't licensed for this, I thought, guzzling down my beer.

Suddenly, Jack looked up at me intently. 'Kitty, what's the worst thing you've ever thought?' he asked.

'The … worst thing I've ever thought?'

Hesitating, I tried to suppress a stab of fear, looking down at the table between us. Jack's eccentricities had shifted gear into mania – his words rapid, his blue eyes darting and suspicious. Why did he need to know about the worst thing I'd ever thought?

'Er, I don't know, to be honest.'

'Come on, the *worst thing*. You've thought bad things, Kitty. We all have.'

Turning on my barstool awkwardly, I looked away from his absurdly intense stare.

'Well, I don't know … sometimes I get annoyed when tourists walk slowly?'

Jack scoffed, and a fresh wave of discomfort washed over me. I wasn't sure what he wanted.

'That can't be the *worst* thing,' he said, looking down at me with a touch of scorn. 'But it's okay, you don't have to tell me.'

'Okay?'

And still I felt too awkward to refuse another drink when he offered. I didn't expect Jack to suggest that we dragged this thing out even longer, and was so thrown off that my mind went blank. Watching him leave for the bar, I slunk off to the bathroom to construct an excuse for leaving after this one: no way would I be caught off-guard again. Thankfully, he saved me the trouble once we'd finished our second round.

'I'm sorry, Kitty. I don't know if you've noticed, but I'm not feeling well tonight,' Jack said, his eyes downcast. 'I feel really anxious, and just … not right.'

'Oh!' I tried not to sound too pleased. 'Well, let's call it a night then. I've got to be up early tomorrow, so don't feel bad.'

Silently, we divided the bill and then finally – *finally* – stepped outside. I closed my eyes for a moment, drawing in a long, sharp breath. The cold rush of evening air was making me feel giddy with relief.

And then suddenly, jarringly, Jack pulled me towards him.

I looked up, baffled. This was the first time he'd touched me all night, and his hold felt rough. Angry. Firmly, Jack gripped my waist, running one hand up the nape of my neck and into my hair, tugging it slightly. In the middle of the busy street, he then dove into a deep, passionate kiss. Part of it felt good; he was, as ever, a good kisser, and the urgency was kind of hot. But mostly it felt weird and embarrassing. Off-kilter.

When he grabbed my arse, my skin prickled. Gently, I broke away, and he looked down at me with disappointment.

'Oh, I wish I felt better tonight, Kitty,' he lamented. 'I'd love to take you home. You don't know how much you're tempting me.'

I smiled up at him blankly. *Tempting him?* I repeated to myself. What was this weird game he was playing? This pointless push and pull? I didn't understand him, and I didn't want to either. Not anymore. I just wanted to go home.

'Don't worry,' I said breezily. 'Hope you feel better soon. I live near Kentish Town, so I'll walk from here.'

'You'll walk?' he parroted, shocked. 'No. No way, I'll walk with you, at least to Kentish Town station.'

And once again, I found myself unable to say no.

Things only got stranger as Jack and I walked. A switch had flipped, and his manically bad mood quickly transformed into an excessively good one. At one point, he actually picked me up in the air and spun me around.

I laughed awkwardly as he put me down, wishing we'd arrive already. Just a few more yards and …

…finally, finally! We reached Kentish Town station.

'Alright, well, I live down there,' I announced, jabbing a thumb at the street corner. 'So I'll be off home now. Nice to see you.'

Well, a white lie couldn't hurt. Or could it? Unhappily, it seemed to give Jack enough encouragement to grab me again. The hair-pulling, arse-grabbing resumed, his tongue snaking around mine in my mouth. Oh God, I thought with rising panic. We were next to a hectic road, outside a busy train station, and my office was a few streets away. I knew for a fact that my colleagues lived nearby – what if they saw me? I felt breathless with embarrassment, desperate to pull away.

Gradually, I lowered myself down from my tiptoes and turned my face to the side. And then all of a sudden Jack's hand was around my throat.

He pulled my mouth back up to his, kissing me hard. It probably only lasted a couple of seconds, but they felt agonisingly slow. I couldn't breathe, and my feet weren't quite on the floor …

Finally, he let go of me and I crumpled back down, looking frantically around for an exit.

'Alright, well,' I said, seizing my bag strap and staring at the road I needed to walk down. Ten minutes from home, I told myself. Just ten minutes from home. 'I'll be off. See you soon.'

Jack sighed heavily in response. 'Oh, Kitty, I'm such an idiot. I wish I could take you home. I'll text you, okay?'

I nodded, then left with a quick wave.

I felt very, very bad on the walk home. Fragmented and nauseous and confused. Like I'd just swallowed something I hadn't asked for.

The badness turned to numbness when I got into bed. I looked up at the ceiling blankly, trying hard to order my thoughts. They seemed to run away as soon as I caught hold of them, though, and I spent the next half hour chasing them around my brain.

Then, when those 30 minutes faded, I felt my chest start to shake. Suddenly I was sobbing, memories of the Bad Thing flooding back. In my mind, I was ten years old again, walking to the edge of a field. I felt strange and violated and small and unfamiliar, like my body didn't belong to me anymore. I existed inside it, but it was alien to me now.

In the present, I held my hands against my face, and wished my fingers could push the tears and overwhelming sadness back in. I hadn't meant to let it out. Black fog started to creep around the fringes of my mind, threatening to trespass further. Not this again, I thought desperately. I'd thought this feeling was behind me. That I was happy now.

My hands were trembling and wet when I took them away, and I placed one loosely on my throat for a moment. I wasn't sure why.

———————

Waking the next morning, I felt groggy and exhausted. What the hell had happened last night?

My body stiff, I sat up in bed and stared at my reflection in the mirror beside me. My face looked strange now, somehow. Tired and worn and crumpled. Desperate for a distraction, I grabbed my phone from the bedside table so that I could mindlessly scroll through Instagram. My stomach lurched as I unlocked it. Jack had messaged last night, asking if I'd got home safe.

Had I *got home safe?*

Oh, I felt sick. I stared down at the message, then fired off a two-word reply: *Yes thanks*. Hopefully that would be it.

Afraid he'd message me back, I left my phone in the bedroom while I showered. I desperately needed a break, I thought. A break from him; a break from everything. Nevertheless, I wondered if I was overreacting, as I massaged shampoo into my scalp. It had been a bad date, yes, but bad dates happened all the time. And I hadn't even wanted to go on it in the first place. Plus, I never had to see him again, whether he replied or not. So why did I care?

Closing my eyes, I suddenly remembered his hand on my throat, pulling me up towards him in public. I turned the water off and opened my eyes, staring at the taps.

Well, it had been passionate at least, a small voice tried to reason. And he was a passionate guy. He even talked about *eating* me at one point. So what had I expected?

Later that morning, Jen knocked on my bedroom door, curious to know how the date had gone.

'Oh. Not good,' I chuckled, towel-drying my hair. 'He was even weirder than last time, if you can believe it.'

'Weirder than "I-want-to-fuck-you-on-the-dancefloor-and-will-you-join-my-religion?"'

'Yeah. Even weirder than that.' I paused, laughing. 'He spent, like, an *hour* talking about himself, and then kissed me like it was the last time he'd kiss anyone in his life.'

She grimaced.

'Yeah. And then,' I added, suddenly hesitant, 'he sort of … grabbed me by the throat as I was leaving? Just outside Kentish Town station.'

My laughter trailed off when I saw her open mouth. Maybe I hadn't overreacted after all, I thought.

When I got to the office, Layla's reaction confirmed that I hadn't.

'Who is he? What's his name?' she demanded. (She's since found her true calling as a police officer.) 'Honestly, mate, you should report him,' she told me from above her monitor.

Shaking my head, I looked back at my own screen in disbelief. I hadn't even considered reporting him to the police – that was way too over the top. 'No, no. I don't think it was that bad,' I protested.

'Honestly, you should,' Layla insisted, shaking her head now as well. 'Or just let me know where he lives so I can go and beat him up. I'm serious, he might do it to someone else.'

Another colleague looked at me with round, sympathetic eyes, and I realised that I'd never be able to spin this into a funny story. I'd never be able to shrug it off or sweep it under the rug. There was no way.

———

Thankfully, Jack and I didn't speak much over the next week – his final week in London. I left it a few days before replying to each message, my stomach flipping every time my phone lit up with a strange link or a: *How are you today?*

When I did, I'd only send two or three words. Unbelievably, I still felt too guilty to ghost him. He might have grabbed me by the throat outside a train station, but I didn't want to be branded a bitch.

The correspondence came to an end when he returned to Ireland, and finally I felt like I could breathe again.

It took me a long time to realise how messed up Jack's behaviour was, which, in itself, says something troubling about what I was willing to expect from casual sex and dating. At the time, I supposed that I'd taken a risk and it hadn't paid off. *Why are you surprised?* my subconscious asked. *You put yourself into the hands of a stranger and he did things to your body you didn't want him to. Big deal. It's a risk of the job.* If I was really hellbent on sleeping around, I had to factor in the possibility of being assaulted.

After all, so many of my single friends had found themselves in situations where they were made to feel uncomfortable. They had all endured times when they felt like they had to go along with things, even as their skin was crawling. They'd been manhandled and manoeuvred and manipulated into shapes that felt strange and upsetting and totally par for the course. It was never a big deal, because you couldn't trust men to behave themselves. Of course you could never hold them to any kind of standard. Boys will be boys, and a girl in a short skirt who fucks before the third date might find herself compromised.

Almost everyone will reinforce this thinking if a strange man hurts you: 'You need to be more careful,' they'll say. 'There are some real weirdos out there, so get to know a guy before you have sex with him. I'm just looking out for you.'

And yet … and yet there was a nagging feeling that this wasn't right. *Surely promiscuous women shouldn't have to factor in the possibility of violence*, a small voice said. And if they did, did I really want to continue down this path?

The beginning of 2019 began to feel like a long, long time ago. I'd set out at the start of the year to experiment with my sexuality, to indulge in the power of owning and exploring it, and yes, I had felt a rush of power while having sex with Jack. But ultimately he'd left me feeling completely disempowered. I was gutted, violated, humiliated. Surely this wouldn't be my experience for the rest of the year?

God, it had better not be. I never wanted to feel like this again, especially at the hands of someone who had briefly made me feel so safe.

The thought made me temporarily hesitant about my new lifestyle. I'd modelled myself after Samantha Jones, but couldn't remember a *Sex and the City* episode where she was grabbed like that in the street. I wondered whether her breeziness about casual sex was an entire work of fiction, inapplicable to real life.

But as the last days of April wore on, I started to rally against this bout of pessimism. Jack was one guy, I told my reflection, which was steadily becoming more familiar. One disrespectful guy who, in all likelihood, had mental health issues he needed to address and work through. It was possible that he was going through something at the time and had acted out of character. This didn't justify his actions, but it did indicate that they were abnormal – that they wouldn't be replicated by the next man I met.

Women should be entitled to fun, carefree, casual sex and, damn it, I'd get mine, I decided. I wouldn't let one man's behaviour put me off.

Months later, I opened my phone to read a final message from Jack. He told me that he was feeling a lot better now, and that leaving London had been good for him. Tentatively, he added that he was thankful he'd spent the last of it with me. And, finally, Jack asked me to look him up if I was ever in Ireland.

No chance, I wanted to reply.

Glad you're feeling better, was what I actually wrote. Then I deleted the chat for good.

CHAPTER 3

Conor

Jen and I moved to a new flat in May. It was a new lease of life, I thought to myself. A new postcode, with new men, although it was W9 – so that probably meant wanky West Londoners.

I counted the chinos on my first wander round Notting Hill. One, two, three, four ... sixteen, seventeen, eighteen.

Brogues were next on the list, but there were too many to count. I gave up and bought a £4 coffee instead, looking around.

Taking pictures with my free hand, I marvelled at ice-cream-coloured houses and prim women walking even primmer little dogs; at stony-faced gardeners trimming luscious box hedges; at tanned men in sunglasses talking on the phone. Stopping for a moment, I gazed up at an imposing pillared house, locked behind cast-iron gates. It was blindingly white in the early summer light, and looked so perfectly soft, as if it was encased in icing.

Suddenly, my phone came alive in my hand. I looked down and saw that Jen was calling.

'Are you at the shops?' she asked.

'No,' I replied, ambling down the road. 'I'm looking for Lily Allen.'

I'd recognised a few spots in her recent Instagram Stories, and was wearing tulle and trainers, which I thought she'd appreciate. Maybe we'd become friends and she'd invite me in for dinner with Adele.

'Well, when you do go, can you get me a bottle of rum?' Jen went on, pulling me back to earth. 'I've run out.'

Unhelpfully, I nodded. We were hosting a housewarming party that evening, so I'd schlep over to Sainsbury's for rum and juice and crisps of various flavours, so long as they were under £2. I'd never held a housewarming party before and suddenly felt very grown up.

I also couldn't wait for my friends to see the flat. After a fairly traumatic search, Jen and I had lucked out. We'd somehow signed for a year in a townhouse in Westbourne Park, a mere *ten-minute walk* from Notting Hill. There were big bay windows in the living room, a blossom tree outside, and ceiling lights which you could actually dim.

I could afford it if it meant saving absolutely nothing each month, so we took it.

The stress didn't end there, however – returning in the form of a trip to IKEA. Giddy with excitement, Jen and I whisked our trolley about the showrooms, throwing in a £3 cocktail glass here, a £1 cushion there, as many £2 plastic plants as we could carry, and somehow ended up with faces as white as the bill we were handed.

'There must be a mistake,' I muttered, running it through my hands. 'He must have scanned something through twice.'

Taking it from me, Jen looked resigned. 'No,' she said remorsefully. 'No mistake. It's all us.'

With pursed lips and wide eyes, we carted our fake creepers home and arranged them in time for the house party. Fucking hell, I thought, looking down at the plastic plants with resentment. They'd better get some compliments.

Nine o'clock came and went, and suddenly the flat was noisy and full. *People had come, people had come!* I sang to myself. And far more than expected! Looking around the living room with dizzy wonder, I thought: 'I've made it. I've finally made it. I'm a metropolitan woman with a swish flat, great friends, regrettable sexual experiences and framed photographs; not a blob of blu-tac in sight.' I was also dizzy because of two glasses of a dubious 'punch' I'd made within the first half hour, which was currently full of satsumas. The recipe suggested you included orange and strawberry slices, but I didn't have either of those and concluded that satsuma slices were just the same. They were the same, weren't they?

Warily, I eyed the baking bowl full of murky orange liquid in the corner of the room and thought: no actually, they are not. That can't be how it's supposed to look. And this couldn't be how it was supposed to taste, I added, looking down at my near-empty glass. Eventually someone approached the bowl with a ladle and accidentally swallowed two pieces of satsuma whole. I blinked as they tried to cover their nose, punch spraying out.

The doorbell rang then and, glad to have an escape, I sprinted downstairs.

'Kitty!' Johnny exclaimed as I opened the door.

'Hooray!' I shouted back.

Johnny was Layla's flatmate and I'd fallen in love with him the first time we met. He spun me around the hallway, my floor-length satin skirt slapping the walls in protest.

'Oh, you know, if I was a straight woman I'd dress *just* like you,' Johnny sighed, putting me down.

I huffed and puffed and blustered, completely unable to process this compliment. A gay man had just told me that if he was a woman he'd dress like me. I could die happily. Following him and Layla inside, I was still reeling. The room couldn't hold my ego, and I couldn't hold my punch.

The party was still going strong at 1 a.m. Most of the guests, including Johnny, had left, but Layla, our friend Maisie and I were hunched in the kitchen around a sticky bottle of whiskey. Knocking back a shot and squeezing her eyes closed, Layla suggested that we take an Uber to Camden Town. We all agreed that this was a brilliant idea. The best idea anyone had ever had.

After this, my memories are patchy. I remember the Uber ride, I remember going to a cashpoint to get £10 out for the bar's entry fee, and I remember dancing and being very, *very* happy, throwing my head back and swishing my skirt about the beer-stained dancefloor. Then I recall ordering a single vodka and coke before being encircled by a group of guys. Actually, I think the more appropriate term would be 'lads'.

One of the 'lads' took me by the waist, and the rest erupted into a chorus of '*wheeey*'s. I was mildly disconcerted when they started filming us on a phone, but too spaced out to care. The music was pounding around my head, this man's fingers digging into my skin. I felt manhandled, but deliciously delirious. And then, all of a sudden, the lights went out.

I'd experienced a blackout once before, when I drank a dirty pint full of vodka, wine, beer and coke at Freshers' Week. But that was seven years ago.

The next thing I remember is lying in the back of a cab with the guy from the bar. The guy I'd been dancing with, I clocked. My limbs felt like jelly, and his arm was somewhere beneath my skirt. My attitude was that of Victoria Beckham at Wimbledon, watching the proceedings with vague interest.

All of a sudden, the cab jolted to a stop.

'Money, we need money,' the man who had just been fingering me said.

'Oh. Okay.' I blinked in quick succession, surprised to find my words slurred. Fumbling around in my purse, I realised that my debit card was no longer there. Even in my inebriated state, a chill ran through me.

'I don't … um … I don't know where my card's gone,' I mumbled.

My companion flew to the rescue, scrambling a note and some coins together and dropping them into the cabbie's hand. I couldn't muster enough sobriety to climb out of the cab, so once again he played the shining knight. I leaned against his chest as he dragged me down the street, screwing my eyes shut and opening them again.

But wait, hang on. Looking around vaguely, I realised that this was my own street. And that was my new front door. Had I given him my address? I wondered. Well, I must have done …

'Come on, where are your keys?'

The strange, auburn-haired man gave me a little shake.

'Oh, yeah.' Once again I rooted around my bag, and this time didn't come up short. Holding my keys in my hand, which also seemed to be made of jelly, something vaguely rational struck me.

'There's nowhere to … you know, by the way,' I told him. 'My friend Anne's in my bed. So there's only the, er, sofa.'

'Well, I'm sure we'll find a bed,' he beamed with entirely misplaced confidence.

Once we were in the flat, I lost the use of my legs again, my heels skittering about on the floor. Auburn-haired man hoisted me up into his arms, once again playing the shining knight.

'Let's go and find your bedroom,' he grinned.

'No-o-o-o.' My voice rose with panic when he made for my room, then Jen's. 'Look,' I slurred, 'it's the sofa-fa, or nothing.'

He looked down at me as if I was joking, then his face dropped.

'Oh! Right. Okay.'

As this strange, red-haired man lowered me onto the sofa, I heard my bag clatter to the ground. He was getting undressed very quickly, I registered, and fiddled with my zipper, attempting to follow suit.

But ugh. My head was cloudy. Strange. I felt like I was on autopilot, but wasn't really sure what I was doing, nor why I was doing it. *Why was I getting undressed with this strange man?* a faint voice asked.

'Chill out,' the man hissed as I pulled at my skirt zipper. But how could I? My arms weren't cooperating. They were wobbly mush and trying to undo my skirt was an impossible feat. This raised other, more pressing questions I wasn't sober enough to answer.

'I ... I can't ...'

I looked up at him helplessly.

Rolling his eyes, auburn-haired man pinned me to the sofa, face-down, and yanked my skirt down for me. Then he wrenched my underwear off. Switching the light off with one hand, he flipped me over onto my back, then rammed himself in.

Oh, fuck.

It didn't last long, but it did hurt. I winced through a few painful pumps and then, mercifully, he came. Relieved it was over, I closed my eyes. And then the blackness descended again.

———————◆———————

There's nothing more sobering than waking up in the cold light of your living room, naked, next to a man wedged into the crevice of a very small sofa.

Suddenly alert, my first panic-stricken thought wasn't: 'Who is this strange man?' It was: 'Fuck. My money. Where's my debit card?'

I turned my purse and bag upside down but no, still no sign of it. Unsure of what else to do, I pressed the home button on my phone, and my stomach dropped.

We have noticed abnormal activity on your account, a text from my bank read. *You withdrew £100 from Chalk Farm Co-op ATM. Was this you? Reply YES or NO.*

NO.

No, no, no.

I lowered my pale face into my hands. I was living in a palace with dimmable lights and had spent the last of my money on rubber creepers from IKEA. I had absolutely no savings. This could *not* be happening.

Thank you, the automated reply read. *Call us to report abnormal activity on your account. Our opening hours are 8 a.m.—8 p.m.*

I checked the time and saw that it was 6 a.m. Fuck. My arm grew limp and I let my phone fall to the ground, though it made my sofa-mate stir.

'Shit,' I muttered at him.

Looking down at his tousled waves, a different wave of panic washed over me.

Motherfucker, I thought, fragmented memories crowding back. He didn't use a condom. We didn't use a condom.

Oh, this was all too much. Way too much at 6 a.m. I pulled a blanket around me and shuffled to my bedroom. Anne was asleep in the bed, and I crawled in next to her, pulling my knees up to my chest. Fucking hell, my head was spinning.

An alarmingly early riser, Anne came back from the kitchen at 8 a.m. to announce that a 'hot, naked man' was asleep on the sofa.

'He looks like um … Archie, from *Riverdale*,' she said.

I chuckled wryly in response, then went back to sleep.

Half an hour later, she got up again to go to the bathroom while I called the bank.

'Hello?' I began, my heart pounding. 'I think someone stole my card.'

I was faint with relief when I hung up a few minutes later, lying back on the bed with a thump. Whoever had taken my card had withdrawn £600 from my account from various ATMs throughout London, but most of it had been blocked. The woman promised that the rest of it would be returned in the course of the day. She was very nice and very reassuring. 'Don't worry, Miss Ruskin,' she said. 'You won't lose any money.'

I heard the door open and sprang up to tell Anne the good news, but stopped when I saw Archie from *Riverdale* at the threshold.

'Ah, so you *do* have a bed,' he noted with delight, wriggling under the covers.

Popping up at the head of the bed, he patted the pillow next to him. 'Come on,' he said, beckoning me over.

Frozen, I stared at him, mouth open, mind blank. 'Er, sure,' I said, moving towards the door. 'I'm just going to, um ... I'm going to the kitchen to grab some water. I'll be right back.'

I met Anne as she left the bathroom and herded her into the living room.

'What are you doing?' she implored. 'I want to go back to bed.'

'You can't,' I hissed. 'The random man from last night is in there. I don't know how to get rid of him. I assumed he'd *leave* after I abandoned him on the sofa.'

She looked unimpressed. 'So I can't go back to sleep?'

'I'm sorry,' I grimaced. 'But maybe ... maybe if we give him half an hour he'll go away.'

They should have a handbook for one-night stands, I thought, massaging my temples as I crumbled down onto the sofa, which I hoped wasn't stained with cum. There should be a whole chapter on how to usher them out the next morning. Why was there no *protocol* to all of this? Or if there was one, how had I missed the memo?

Making ourselves useful while we waited, Anne and I cleared last night's bottles away. Thirty minutes later, I creaked open the bedroom door and peered in. Archie was still there, flat against my mattress and fast asleep, one pasty leg draped over the covers.

'Maybe just another half an hour?' I suggested, returning to the living room sheepishly.

Anne shook her head. 'Kitty, get that man out of your bed right now.'

Shuffling back into my bedroom, I tweaked the curtains open, shafts of light poking through. Then I reached for my dressing gown and 'fell' into the dresser.

'Whoops,' I said, almost pantomime-like.

It worked. Gently, Archie stirred. 'Oh, hey,' he mumbled, looking up at me with a lazy, handsome smile.

'Hi. So, look …' I paused, sitting down on the edge of the mattress. 'I'm so sorry, but I'm actually heading out to meet a friend for brunch. Is that okay?'

'For brunch? You and …? Oh.' Archie's face fell as he registered my meaning. 'Yeah, sure. That's fine. I'll head off.'

To my dismay, 'heading off' seemed to mean crawling to the foot of the bed and sitting down next to me.

'What's your name, by the way?' he asked.

I threw him an impatient look, desperate to hurry this along.

'Kitty.' I bit my lip then, mildly appalled that I'd had sex with a nameless stranger. 'What's yours?'

'Conor. Wait a second though, is that your real name?'

'Yeah.'

Conor smirked.

'Oh, okay. Ha. That's a cool guitar,' he added, grinning.

'Er, thanks.' I looked at Conor again curiously. It was as if I was seeing him – *really* seeing him – for the first time. He looked young. Very young. And the way he'd been talking just now … he didn't sound older than 20.

'How old are you?' I asked hesitantly.

Conor's eyes darted away. 'Well, how old are *you*?' he countered.

'No, no. You first.'

'I'm, um … 22.'

My shoulders sank. 'Oh, thank goodness,' I sighed. Then I eyed him again, somewhat suspiciously. 'You have a very young face.'

He smiled and shrugged, saying nothing.

Eventually Conor left, but getting rid of him was like pulling teeth. First he couldn't find his socks, then he couldn't find his belt. Then he sat down at the table to show me photos of his squadron.

'We're all here in London for my friend's stag do,' he told me. 'I've never been here before.'

'Oh, right,' I replied, cupping my chin.

'It's a lot bigger than I thought it'd be. And the pollution? The pollution's bad.'

'I suppose so, yeah.'

'When you blow your nose it's all black. Did you know that?'

'Yeah, I think I've heard that happens.'

Finally, after thanking me for having him – twice – Conor stepped out into the hallway. I closed the door behind him and rested my forehead against it for a moment. At last, at last – what a relief. But ow, my head was still spinning.

Oh, this was a low point.

I was a walking hangover, heading to Boots for the morning-after pill with a very large minus sign in my account. I'd waited all day for the remaining £300 to return to me, but it hadn't. When I called the bank again, the woman from this morning was nowhere to be found. In her place was a taciturn Welshman who, despite his accent, was no comfort at all.

He asked me what kind of bag I'd been wearing, how drunk I'd been, and how it was possible that the thief knew my PIN number.

'I have no idea,' I replied, exasperated.

'Is it possible that someone you know might have stolen it?' he asked, twirling a small, black moustache, I imagine.

'No.' I stared at the floor. 'Someone must have looked over my shoulder when I was using the ATM, I guess.'

'Were you shielding your PIN?'

'No.' A bit hard, when your hands are made of jelly.

'Well, do always shield your PIN in future, Miss Ruskin,' the man instructed, with all the gravitas of a head teacher.

'Right. Yes. Will do. So, what about the rest of my money?'

'I'm afraid you'll need to file a report with the police and, if they decide to investigate, we'll arrange for the money to be returned to you.'

'And if they don't?'

'Well, I'm sorry, Miss Ruskin, but there's just no way to prove that it wasn't you making these withdrawals.'

'Me?' I squeaked. 'Making withdrawals of £600 from various cashpoints, throughout London, in the early hours of the morning? Does that sound like a standard Saturday night to you?'

'I'm sorry, Miss Ruskin, but there's nothing I can do.' His tone was final.

So, yes, this was bleak. The morning-after pill cost £30, and required me to squeeze onto a very hard chair, in a very small room, opposite a man who asked me when 'the incident' had occurred.

£330 into my overdraft, I returned home and lay flat on my bed, which now smelt a little of Lynx Africa.

———————————

Two days later, still bereft, I received a call from Lydia at my desk. She had good news.

She knew someone who worked for a newspaper and he had a contact at the bank. He said I was entitled to get my money back, and that he'd call the contact and ask for a quote, telling them he was writing a story on it.

The next day, a smooth-toned woman called me to apologise. She apologised up and down the British Isles, in fact.

'But, as an apology isn't enough, are you happy for me to deposit £100 compensation into your account?'

I told her that I was happy for her to do this, and returned to my desk with a spring in my step. I'd actually made a profit from the debacle.

'And all I had to do was have sex with a 22-year-old,' I gloated.

'Twenty-two?' Layla looked up at me and barked a laugh. 'You do realise he wasn't 22?'

I stared at her.

'He was nineteen,' she said. 'His friends told me they all were.'

'No,' I breathed. 'Oh my God. I'm a cougar.'

For the ninth time that week, I lowered my head into my hands.

A couple of days later, I was watching the street below my bus window when I realised that I was bleeding. Heavily.

Oh, shit. *Really* heavily. I dashed off at the next stop and straight into the office toilets – no time for a morning coffee; no time to say hello to Brian at reception. I charged straight past him and into a cubicle.

Wow. Okay, yeah. There was a *lot* of blood. Peeling off the liner I'd put in just in case (I was warned to expect spotting after taking the morning-after pill), I saw that it had soaked all the way through. Dabbing my underwear with a lump of tissue, I wondered what this meant. I hadn't bled through since I was sixteen, and wasn't due for a couple of weeks. Yes, the morning-after pill could make your period come early, but this was very early and *very* heavy. Was that normal?

Briefly shaking my head, I grabbed two sanitary towels from my bag and decided to put it out of my mind. I was fine, probably.

An hour later, I wasn't so sure. I was struggling to focus on my computer screen. My vision kept shifting in and out of focus. On top of that I felt weak; groggy, like I was about to fall down at any given moment. It didn't help that blood was gushing out of me like Niagara bloody Falls. Pun not intended.

I could only withstand it for so long, so I grabbed my phone and scuttled off to the stairwell at the earliest opportunity. Then I sat and closed my eyes with my head between my knees and thought, 'What the hell is happening? Am I dying?' My right hand shaking, I called 111 and said: 'Hello, I'm bleeding heavily and I feel like I'm about to faint. I'm not sure if that's, er, normal?'

111 transferred me to my GP, where a kindly but insistent doctor asked me if 'there was any chance I could be pregnant'.

The question hit me like a tonne of bricks. Suddenly, it felt like something was lodged in my throat. 'Yes, I suppose there is,' I said hesitantly. 'But I ... I took the morning-after pill. So I don't think it's very likely? Or even possible, is it?'

'O-kay.' There was that gentle insistence again. 'Kitty, it might be a bad reaction to the morning-after pill, and if that's the case, you're fine – just take it easy today,' he said. 'But we need to rule out that you're pregnant first, alright? If you are, you need to go to A&E immediately. Do you understand?'

I wasn't sure I did understand.

'Yes,' I faltered.

'Alright, are you at home?'

'No,' I said, my voice distant, as if someone else was speaking. The word seemed to float up out of my body, independent of my brain. 'I'm at work.'

'Fine. You need to go home now and take a pregnancy test, and if you're pregnant, go to A&E immediately. If you're not, it's probably just a bad reaction to the morning-after pill, okay?'

'Okay.' No, no, no. This was *not* okay. The stairwell was swimming around me, and I couldn't feel my legs.

Somehow, I mustered enough strength to return to my desk, snatch my bag and dart out to the nearest pharmacy, where I bought a pregnancy test with tears in the corners of my eyes. This was so fucking weird. I couldn't be pregnant, I thought desperately. Could I? Surely not. Nineteen-year-old Conor couldn't have gotten me pregnant. There was no way.

Even more pressingly, was I having a miscarriage right now?

I'm aware now that I couldn't have known if I was pregnant with Connor's baby a couple of days after sex, and that it wouldn't have shown on a test, but my sex education had been so limited that I didn't know this at the time. As a result, my thoughts were racing when I sat down on the bus. If I'm pregnant, I'm going to save you, little baby, I found myself thinking, placing two protective hands on my stomach. But I couldn't afford a baby, and Conor – being nineteen – couldn't afford one either. Maybe if I told Jack it was his, he could help me provide for it, I thought. It? Her? Him?

Oh shit, I was properly crying now. No, I couldn't be pregnant.

As soon as I reached home, I dropped my bag and slammed the bathroom door behind me. Still woozy, my hands rattling,

I bent down, peed on a stick and waited with a hammering heart for the result. Minutes later, it came.

Not pregnant, it said.

Not pregnant!

'Oh, thank God,' I breathed, collapsing onto the side of the bath.

Tears of relief were spilling down my face. Thank God, thank God, thank God, I mouthed to myself. Staring up at the ceiling, I let the tears fall out with a long, shuddering breath. Then I tossed the test into the bin.

Filling a hot water bottle, I stepped out of my skirt and into bed, pulling the duvet around my body and willing this morning to end. Drifting off, a final thought occurred to me: I couldn't believe I'd considered telling Jack he was the father.

***

Even after that dreadful morning, for a long time Conor was just another story to tell at parties. An extra £100. For months, that night was a funny anecdote until suddenly, very suddenly, it wasn't.

One sun-soaked Saturday I was going out shopping, smiling as I stepped through Notting Hill. I was excited about buying a dress for the summer, and then all of a sudden I was crying. Crying openly in the street. Bewildered, I put my hands to my cheeks, wet with tears, and screwed my eyes shut.

I shook my head, but it didn't help. I couldn't shake the flashbacks of Conor fucking me. Conor on top of me. My limp limbs in the dark. They were pouring into my mind like molten lava.

Oh, I'm going mad, I thought, vomit at the back of my throat. Why was this happening? Why was I reacting like this?

Months after that sunny Saturday, I came to the difficult conclusion that I'd been raped. There were a few reasons why it took me so long to reach this conclusion. One: rape culture. Just think of the movies we watched growing up: *Sixteen Candles*, for instance, in which the jock tells the nerd that he's 'got Caroline in the bedroom right now, passed out cold. I could violate her ten different ways if I wanted to.' Looking at him disparagingly, the nerd retorts: 'What are you waiting for?' But instead of violating her himself, the jock charitably gives the sleeping Caroline to the nerd in exchange for another woman's underwear. 'I'm only a freshman,' says the nerd. The reply comes quickly. 'So? She's so blitzed she won't know the difference.'

Or *The 40-Year-Old Virgin*, for a more recent example, in which the virgin's colleague tells him that the easiest way to get laid is to search bars for inebriated girls. 'Drunk chicks,' he specifies. 'Don't confuse that with tipsy. We're talking about drunk. I want vomit in the hair. Bruised-up kneecaps. Broken heels is a plus.'

Yes, things have changed now. And no, those movies probably wouldn't have featured those scenes post-#MeToo. Still, there was a time when this mentality was prevalent; when taking advantage of drunk girls wasn't unusual. It was 'naughty' or 'cheeky' at worst – just another instance of 'boys being boys'. And we've all internalised that mentality to some degree. I certainly had.

My mind was also slow to accept that my body had been raped because of self-defence. After something traumatic happens, you don't *want* to acknowledge that it's happened. You don't feel ready to face it, or capable of admitting it. That's why I feel angry when I see comments online about it 'taking so long' for victims to come forward, as if that negates their claim. It can take weeks or months or years before you're even cognisant of the fact that you've been raped. People who haven't experienced rape will never know this, but it doesn't make it less true.

Thirdly, I didn't want to admit that I'd been raped because that would *definitely* mean I had failed in my mission to have a year of fun, carefree, casual sex. The cracks in my plan had started to show with Jack, and I didn't want Conor to widen them further. I wanted to believe that women *could* have casual sex in 2019 without the threat of rape or assault. That they could be as liberated and as fearless as they liked. The alternative was too bleak to consider.

Finally, I didn't want to let the black fog encroach further. I'd struggled with depression and anxiety for much of my life, but was determined not to let it ruin it. I *would* be happy, I told myself. I *would* enjoy my life. I wouldn't go back to crying on bathroom floors and thinking about killing myself, as I had done in years prior. Those long, nauseating hours were behind me. I wouldn't let them come back. To keep them at bay, I pushed the awful truth down.

Ultimately, however, I couldn't ignore that Conor had raped me. There came a point when I could no longer sweep it to the side, repackaging my trauma as a more palatable anecdote.

The fact is, it *wasn't* okay that Conor fucked me when I couldn't walk. It wasn't okay for him to drag me down the street, to shake me to unlock my door and to carry me through my house. It wasn't okay for him to aggressively pound me without a condom when I had no command over my arms and legs. And it wasn't okay that I had to sit on a hard chair at the pharmacy the next day and hand over money for being raped.

And why had I blacked out, anyway? I found myself wondering.

A year later, I chewed the inside of my mouth while I watched *I May Destroy You*, uncomfortable because, shit, it felt so familiar. The dancing, the blackout, the coming to, the fuzzy aftermath.

Had I been drugged that night? I asked myself. I still don't know, and never will. I do find it strange that I blacked out after four cocktails, a shot and a single vodka and coke, and lost all control of my legs. But regardless of whether I was drugged or just drunk, the fact is that a man had sex with me when I had no power to consent. And, years later, I still feel violated.

Angry, too. So fucking angry. How *dare* he do this to me? To anyone? And sit in my house afterwards as if nothing had happened?

Sometimes that white-hot feeling is hard to deal with – it bursts into flames in my chest, stretching up into my throat. I can almost hear the fierceness of the fire as it rushes up into my ears. It makes me feel violent. It makes me feel out of control. And there's nowhere for that rage to go. At the end of the day, he's a stranger who did an awful thing and then disappeared into the daylight, facing zero consequences, zero vengeance, zero justice.

Even worse than the anger is the anguish.

A friend once told me that you lose a part of yourself every time you get raped, and I think I lost a part of myself that evening. A little bit of innocence was chipped away; a little more peace sucked out into the night.

I'm still struck down by the sadness of it sometimes. The other day I was walking by the canal on my lunch break, and

I stopped to stare at the white sky above me. My thoughts quiet, I looked up at it, blank like a piece of paper, laid out perfectly flat. I listened to the seagulls cry out in the distance, watching their bodies wheel around in the autumn wind, and closed my eyes, bracing for a fresh wash of grief.

Tears stung as the memories rushed back. They always flood back violently, like water bursting from a pipe.

How could he go on forgetting while I went on remembering? I asked the white sky. *And when would the remembering stop?*

CHAPTER 4

Leo

As I said, it took months to process the fact that I'd been raped. Because of this, I had no immediate hesitations about dating, post-Conor. Perhaps there was a part of me, too, that wanted to rebel against the victim status I was faintly cognisant of, deep down. It was the same urge that made me label myself as 'frigid and awkward' when I was a virgin, rather than 'broken by a traumatic experience that happened when I was ten'.

Being a victim isn't sexy. Being a victim isn't fun. By continuing to go on dates, I felt that I was shaking off the chains of victimhood, proving that I could and *would* have enjoyable, consensual sex. That I was capable and deserving of it. This could be my sparky, lighthearted year of debauchery yet. There was still time. I could still go out and have empowering sex with strangers.

Somewhere buried in my subconscious, I also started to crave a very particular kind of stranger. Someone kind and gentle; someone who would loosen his hold and ask if I was okay if I started to look panicked. I was still only looking for casual sex, but I wanted to have it with someone who was almost painfully respectful. Someone who was warm and sweet and easy and safe.

Leo's first Hinge message featured a sunflower emoji, and this seemed to hint that he might be such a stranger. Looking down at the little flower in my hand, I decided that it was whimsical, sensitive.

Clicking through to his profile, I zoomed in on the first picture, his handsome, weather-beaten face creasing around a Colgate smile. In his early thirties, Leo had an illustrious career in photography and a head of short, auburn curls. I laughed at the selfie with a goat, and matched.

Within the hour, we were chatting. It was the sort of conversation that reduces you to a smirking teenager, lying flat on your bed, legs swinging behind you. Gently flirtatious, his messages seemed intelligent, considered and colourful. Time and time again, he'd punctuate them with a sunflower emoji. It was charming.

The next day, Leo and I agreed on a night when we were both free, and I told him I'd meet him in Soho.

Before I left the house, I heaped my entire wardrobe onto the bed, rooting through strappy dresses, tired T-shirts and ripped tights I should have thrown out long ago. Eventually I settled on a black turtleneck and a fitted, leopard-print skirt. Twisting in front of my full-length mirror, I registered that I was more self-conscious than usual. Leo was just *so* good looking, I worried that he was a touch out of my league. Dating someone better looking was fine if you were a guy ('Get in! Go on my son,' your friends would say), but if you were a girl, it was widely considered to be embarrassing (*someone else is more attractive than you? Get in the Thames*).

Leaving the station at Tottenham Court Road, I scrunched up an old tissue in my jacket pocket, feeling anxious. On top of my sudden dip in confidence, I hated meeting people in Soho, with its maze of streets and jostling, angry people. It was impossible to make out the restaurant names for all the clamouring crowds, and cars kept creeping up behind me and beeping.

Finally, I spotted a head of auburn, and Leo turned round to smile at me.

Oh, shit. He was even better looking in person.

'We should have booked somewhere,' he grinned as I approached. Then he pulled me in for a hug, which felt surprisingly intimate. My face against his black shirt, I breathed in his aftershave: smokey and rugged, but soft. Subtle.

I agreed as I pulled away, craning my neck to see the restaurant queue snaking around a corner. 'Shall we go somewhere else?'

He looked at me sceptically. 'We could try.'

Taking his hand, I followed Leo through the crowds – in and out of restaurants that were all fully booked. 'It'll be a half-hour wait,' the fourth waitress warned, leaving us by her podium.

'Well?' Leo rubbed my shoulder.

'Yeah, waiting's fine,' I smiled back at him. 'I think we'll have to admit defeat.'

He nodded, and we settled on two barstools by a shelf in the hallway, hassled waiters turboing past us. As Leo disappeared to get our drinks, I peered into the bustling restaurant down the hall, taking a moment to bask in my good luck. This man was unbelievably attractive, with his long legs and big hands and jewel-like eyes. I could feel myself blushing – how embarrassing! – and pressed my cool hands to my face.

Returning from the bar with two small, expensive drinks, Leo plonked mine down on the shelf and beamed at me. Oof, I thought. I could sunbathe in that smile.

'So, how's your day been?' he opened.

'Yeah, pretty busy … I'm glad it's the weekend. How was yours?'

'Oh, the same really.'

God, our chat was awkward at first – crammed, as we were, into a narrow hallway with people careering back and forth. And he kept looking at the candle by my elbow for some reason. Finally, Leo reached around me, picked it up, and set it down by the front door.

'Sorry,' he said, returning with a red face. 'I'm just nervous. Jittery. I didn't want you to catch on fire. Heh.'

Chuckling as well, I stared at him in disbelief. *Leo* was nervous? *Leo* was blushing? Well, this was a turn up for the books! My ego ballooning, I tried to put him at ease.

I shrugged. 'Wouldn't be my worst first date.'

'God. So the bar is low?'

You have no idea, I thought, sipping my cocktail.

'Well, anyway,' Leo smiled, 'I was worried it would be our last.'

I blinked at him, my mouth still on the rim of my glass. The sweetness of the sentiment had caught me off guard. And the more I looked up at his frank, earnest face, the more I felt my shoulders sink. He was so handsome, yet so gentlemanly. And so smitten, apparently. Well, this was *great*.

Things only got more promising when we were taken to our table. Leo's face softened when he spoke about his younger sisters. He made me laugh with a story about geese I wish I could remember. He told me about a documentary he'd been watching the night before, without patronising me or mansplaining along the way. (I'd found, in my brief history of dating, that this happened an awful lot. Apparently, as a woman, you have to be prepared to have documentaries explained to you. Especially if, like me, you hadn't seen a single Louis Theroux. On my first date with Jack he'd asked if I'd seen any good documentaries lately, and I'd floundered and replied, '*The March of the Penguins*'.)

Anyway, I tried not to imagine Leo in a tux when he ordered our third round of drinks. He was a cookie-cutter version of a man. Shiny, faultless.

After a couple of hours we left the restaurant, upping sticks to a pub nearby. It was the kind of Victorian pub tourists and seedy old men flock to, with inky black counters, glowing lanterns and a cobbled road outside.

I ordered a large red wine, sipped it, and stared up again at Leo. His eyes looked kind in the warm light, specks of gold dancing in his irises.

Nursing our drinks, we carried on talking though we knew it didn't matter anymore – every sentence presented itself like a bridge to a kiss. I watched his mouth open and close, his body inching nearer with each reply. My neck felt hot, my hands a little clammy.

At last, Leo said: 'I love your funny face. I want to kiss it.' And he leaned forward, our lips finally meeting.

It was a deep, tender kiss. I held onto the countertop with one hand, my knees wobbling slightly.

Thirty minutes later we'd PDA'd most of the old-timers out of the room. Winding a blonde curl of mine around his finger, Leo suggested that we go back to my flat.

Turning my head, I faltered, laughing awkwardly into the crook of his neck. Up until this point, there had been something romantic and old-fashioned about Leo. Sexy as well, but fiercely respectful. He'd wrapped me up in his wholesome world of funny stories and family holidays and movies that made him cry. Wanting to knock boots on the first date wasn't in keeping with this image …

'Ha. Not tonight,' I said uncertainly.

A few minutes later, the bartender rang his bell with gusto, and Leo and I stepped outside. The air was cool, a summer's sky languishing above us. Velvety and midnight blue. I stretched my arms out, tipsy and happy.

'Well, I'm going back to Tottenham Court Road,' I told Leo brightly. 'Where are you heading?'

Leaning down, he took my face in both of his hands, kissing me again.

'Come on,' he whispered into my ear conspiratorially. 'Take me with you.'

I paused, discomfort encroaching on my happiness. I didn't want to say no to Leo – I really liked him. Yes, I was only looking for something casual, but I wanted to see him more than once. I didn't want to say no if it would jeopardise my chances of seeing him again, and I didn't want to ruin the night …

I didn't think much about how pushy he was being about sex. I couldn't, because he was just so *nice*. So gentlemanly. So unbelievably perfect. I'd be insane, wouldn't I, to say no to Leo?

With my gentle nod he took my hand and pulled me down the street. We giggled as we made it onto the

tube – just – and sank down next to each other. His hand
on my knee and his thumb behind my ear, Leo kissed me
fervently – the other passengers looking on with bemused
expressions. Glancing down the carriage, I saw a woman
roll her eyes.

We hardly spoke on the journey back to Westbourne Park.
He continued kissing me, his large hands inching towards my
hemline. And when we arrived, I felt him grip the back of my
waist as we approached the ticket barriers, more or less pushing me through.

Unsurprisingly, it was straight to business when I closed
the bedroom door behind us. Leo tugged his clothes off with
vigour, then mine. Lying back on the bed (which I'd cleared
before leaving, thank God), I tried to swallow my shock when
he pulled down his pants. Standing to attention, his penis
was the size of a small country. I imagined a megabus going
down an alleyway, and paled. To my intrigue, it was also bent
slightly down the middle. Was it … wonky?

I didn't have long to dwell on this. Grabbing both of my
legs below the knee, Leo pinned them next to my head and
started thrusting, hard and fast. Sweat fell from his reddening brow onto my bare chest, and he pressed against my legs
harder.

Fucking hell … I winced, feeling a bit like origami. It
didn't hurt exactly, but one of my legs started getting pins
and needles, and I wasn't sure if the noises I was making were
born out of discomfort or pleasure. This was some strange,
hazy hinterland, I thought. I'd definitely wanted him, but not
like this.

Finally, Leo freed my legs and turned me over. I was
relieved to find the feeling flood back into them, but there
was a problem. In this position, whether because of the angle

of his penis or his own frantic misdirection, Leo kept slipping out. Time and time again.

I sensed his mounting frustration and embarrassment after a few moments, and grimaced at the wall. Maybe we should just call it a day, I wanted to say. I'll put on Netflix and you can give your bendy penis a break. But with a grunt, Leo heaved to insert himself one final time. Then I felt his body go lax.

Gently, he pulled himself back out. I froze on all fours, staring at the indentations in the wallpaper. Was that it, then? I wondered. Had he given up?

And then, all of a sudden, I felt him go back in – just not into my vagina this time.

'Oh!'

I blinked in shock. What the fuck! Prince Charming was doing me up the arse.

It goes without saying that I'd never had anal sex before. Thankfully, it didn't hurt. But even in my foggy, mid-fuck brain, I couldn't believe that he hadn't asked me first.

Still, I let it play out. It wasn't good, but it wasn't horrible, either. And at least I could feel my legs.

Leo pulled me into a tight embrace after he came, still quivering. Then he stroked my hair until I fell asleep.

In the early morning light he carried on caressing and petting me, one hand moving up and down my forearm, the other massaging my back.

'Good morning,' he whispered when I stirred, squeezing the back of my neck.

Turning to look into Leo's kind eyes, I thought about how unreasonable it was to feel weird about last night. Yes, he'd had aggressive sex with me on our first night together. And no, he hadn't asked before doing me up the arse. But he was so sweet, so attentive. And men loved anal, everybody knew that. They all wanted to do it. I couldn't blame him for giving into that very natural urge, with no time to check whether it was okay with me.

With a cursory stroke of my face, Leo sprang up and out of bed.

'I've got a camping trip with friends in an hour,' he explained, yanking on his jeans. 'So I need to run home and pack.'

'Oh,' I said, staring at his rapidly moving limbs. 'Okay.'

Checking my phone for the time, my heart sank. Was he really just going to up and leave at 8 a.m? Looking up, I watched him fasten his belt buckle, feeling peeved and slightly humiliated.

'Well, I'll see you to the door,' I said vaguely.

'Ha! Don't worry. I'm sure I can find it myself,' Leo grinned. And with a peck goodbye he was gone.

Hearing his footsteps grow faint, I went to the bathroom and stared at the tiled floor. I couldn't join the two men together – the sensitive man who I'd shared my pad thai with and the one who had surprised me with anal, then promptly disappeared. I shook my head, again convincing myself that this was a good, nice, handsome man. I'd had a good night, hadn't I? I asked myself. The sex had been fun, hadn't it? Well, sort of …

And I wanted to see him again, right?

The sad truth was that: yes, I did want to see him again. I couldn't let go of the fantasy of Leo – the beautiful photographer who took me by the hand in Soho and told me about his sisters. He still seemed to hold so much potential, and perhaps the surprise anal was a brief discrepancy, not representative of his character or of his general behaviour. Maybe he'd never do it again.

Maybe I could have more magical dates with Leo. Maybe the sex would get better, more respectful.

So I was put out when Leo didn't message me the next day. Or the next day, or the next. I would finally hear from him again two weeks later. Back in Soho, I was crossing the road to go and meet a friend for coffee when my phone lit up in my hand.

How you doing, kid? Leo asked. **Sunflower emoji**.

God, I was ashamed to feel my heart lift. But in an instant my first impression of him came flooding back. That faultless, funny man, smiling at me over dinner.

A little reticent, I replied. He asked if I was free later.

Not tonight, sorry.

Why? What are you doing? Leo probed.

Going to a friend's for dinner.

I felt a stab of guilt for lying. Still, although I'd replied to him, there was a nagging voice in my head that said I shouldn't see him again. He'd surprised me with anal and disappeared for days – it wasn't rocket science that going out to meet him again would be a bad idea. I had to stay strong, I told myself. I had to be aloof.

Back to his old pushy ways, however, Leo wouldn't let up.

Come and see me afterwards. There's a great jazz bar I know you'd love. I'd really, really love to see you tonight, Kitty x.

Staring down at my phone, I did a double take in disbelief. Was he actually *begging* to meet? I wrestled with the prospect of giving in for a few minutes, then asked if I could let him know later.

At 5.30 p.m. I unlocked my phone to two back-to-back texts, sent ten minutes apart. *Hey, have you decided yet?* the first one read. *Decided yet?* the next one parroted.

Oh, fuck it, I thought with a sigh. Unlocking my front door, I padded into the kitchen and slid a pizza into the oven, pouring a large glass of wine.

Yes, tonight sounds good, I replied, ashamed but fizzing with excitement. *Where do you want to meet?*

After eating I showered, shaved my legs, and reapplied a full face of makeup. Then, at 7.30 p.m., I sat in my towel and stared down at my phone in confusion. What had it been now, two hours? I wondered. Two hours, and he still hadn't replied. Another twenty minutes passed and I shook my head, water dripping onto the carpet. Fearing the worst, I changed into pyjamas rather than the tight skirt beckoning me from the bed. Another hour passed, and my fears proved valid.

Well and truly humiliated, I wiped off my foundation and tried not to catch my own eye in the mirror. Oh, I was an idiot.

The world felt quiet. Shell-shocked in sympathy. After begging to meet me, Leo had ghosted me. I just ... couldn't believe it. Sinking into the sofa, *Friends* playing in front of me, I looked down at my smooth legs and cringed.

Over the next few days, I would complain to anyone who would listen. Friends had their theories. Lizzie broached the idea that he had a secret girlfriend; Lydia thought that picking me up and dropping me had given him some thrill. Personally, I think he had a rolodex of people who might fuck him, and some other poor soul had beaten me to the punch.

It's very sobering – realising that you don't know someone at all. That your initial idea of them had been just that, an idea. All of Leo's quirks and stories and heartfelt words had been nothing more than smoke and mirrors. Letters spoken like a password. A tried and tested code to get someone into bed.

But what *was* this? I asked myself in frustration. This year was supposed to be me being a female Lothario; me trading one guy for another with impunity. With the exception of Joel, why did I keep getting taken in and screwed over by guys? Why were they always the ones in control?

Another fortnight passed and, like clockwork, Leo got back in touch. Sitting on the top deck of the bus, I looked down at his message and nearly laughed.

Hello lovely, how are you? he asked. **Sunflower emoji**.

I thought about all the things I could say to him, but decided to leave the flower on read. What a bloody sociopath, I thought, sliding my phone back into my pocket. I'd never trust a 'perfect guy' again.

———————

But I would, months later, in February of the following year. I saw this guy for a much longer stretch of time than I saw Leo, and every aspect of his personality suggested that he was genuinely thoughtful and earnest and kind.

On our fourth date, however, I found myself in a familiar position: on all fours, a penis being inserted somewhere I didn't want it to go. He didn't check that I was okay with it, either. He didn't discuss it with me first.

Firmer this time, I pulled away from him, but he kept pushing his penis back in. He tried to coerce me into anal sex four times before he finally gave in to vaginal penetration.

And I felt bad about that coercion, days later. Ever so slightly violated.

Months later I sat at the table in my living room window, turning a cup of tea in my hand. I felt choked up suddenly, tears pooling in the sides of my eyes, the memory of this guy and Leo crowding back into my mind. Putting the mug down, I lifted my phone and googled: 'Guy wouldn't stop having anal sex with me'. The search results were wall-to-wall porn links, with titles like 'Guy has anal with girl until she cries' and 'Boyfriend forces girlfriend to have anal sex'.

Agog, I kept scrolling until I found a link which wasn't porn. At last I came to a Quora message board, where an anonymous girl had written: 'I had casual sex with a guy last night and he pushed me into doing anal. I feel really weird about it now. But I don't know whether I should? Am I overreacting?'

The first response came back as a bark. 'You had casual sex with a guy and wanted him to treat you as anything other than a porn star? That's not how the world works. If you act like a slut, you'll be treated like one. Wise up.'

What the fuck?

Swallowing my horror, I locked my phone and turned it face-down on the table. Was this really how some people thought? I wondered. Did people really think that a woman having casual sex should expect a night which made her feel violated, just as I'd subconsciously told myself after Jack? Did people really think that it was a risk of the job? Closing my mouth, I stared outside.

How on earth was this the status quo? I appealed to the silent postie in the street. And how was I supposed to have casual sex in a society like this?

For weeks, I turned this internet man's words over in my head. Particularly the bit about 'being treated like a porn star'. The search results echoed this sentiment – that perhaps the problem started with porn. And then I read an interview in *The Times* which struck a chord. An interview with Soma Sara, the founder of Everyone's Invited – an online movement committed to tackling rape culture.

'[Porn] reinforces boys' idea of entitlement over women's bodies, with consent not even existing in porn,' she said. 'It's very toxic, yet it's ingrained at such a young age – 11-year-old boys are watching porn. That's their sex education. Sex education should be treated with the same interest as an academic subject, but [while I was at school] it was a joke.'

Sitting back in my chair, I recalled my own pitiful sex education, remembering how our classroom had erupted into sniggers over a cartoon about condoms. We'd learnt about putting them on; about why it was absolutely essential to wear them to prevent the catastrophe of teenage pregnancy, but that was it, wasn't it? There was no lesson about consent. No suggestion that you should ask for it before inserting yourself into someone. No indication that you should even take an interest in what your partner was or wasn't comfortable with.

My stomach sank as I reread the interview. I worried that Soma was right: that prepubescent boys were getting their sex education from the extreme, problematic world of porn, and that this education was trickling into their attitudes as adults.

I wonder if either Leo or the other guy even entertained the idea that they had done something wrong, and I seriously doubt it. It doesn't excuse either incident, but it speaks to an issue much broader than 'they were just bad guys'. The problem is more far-reaching, more insidious; lodged deep in a web of misogyny we're still unable to untangle ourselves from.

If the 'nice guys' are pushing us into sex we don't want, what are the 'bad ones' doing?

At the start of 2019, I'd expected to learn all sorts of interesting things about myself and my own sexuality. And here I was, learning all sorts of things I didn't want to know about male sexuality. This was not part of the plan.

CHAPTER 5

Owen

A few weeks after Leo, Lizzie and I were hungover in a café courtyard, sunglasses sliding down our noses in the heat.

'I think the issue is my taste in men,' I said, watching her drink her coffee.

'Well, I can believe that.'

'So what's wrong with me? Do you think I keep going for fuckboys?'

'Fuckboys?' I could just about see Lizzie squint behind her lenses. 'To be honest with you, I'm not really sure what fuckboys are.' She paused. 'Is that what you think Leo was?'

'Yeah. Either that, or ...' I reached for the sugar. 'Or maybe a softboy?'

'Oh, God. Now you've really lost me. And don't draw me another chart, that won't help.'

I laughed, remembering the softboy/fuckboy/e-boy/e-girl square I'd drawn her on a napkin the night before.

'You could just say "arsehole",' she grumbled. 'That was a good enough word for a long time.'

Nodding, I glanced across the courtyard at a tanned blonde kissing her friend, who was dressed in a shapeless cotton dress and eating half an avocado on toast. Maybe Lizzie had a point, I thought. From that picture to our discussion of fuckboys, this was becoming grotesquely millennial.

'He was an *arsehole* then, yes,' I said self-consciously. 'As was Jack. I just want to date someone nice for a change, you know. Just for a bit of ...' I waved my hands in no particular direction. 'For a bit of variation.'

'Well, there are nice guys out there,' Lizzie said brightly, ever the optimist. 'Maybe you just need to broaden your horizons. Date a few different people.'

'Or lower my standards.' I sighed, looking down at the table glumly. 'I feel like all the good-looking ones are bastards, you know? Maybe because men are already self-entitled enough. Add good looks to that, and they act like the world is their bloody oyster. Because it is. To attractive men the world is one gargantuan oyster.'

I ended this rant with a frown, hoping I wasn't becoming bitter.

'Well, yeah, looks aren't everything,' Lizzie conceded, cutting up the last of her pancake. 'I'd take a cute guy with a nice personality over a model any day. You know, if given the choice,' she added with a chuckle.

I paused, absorbing this information as I watched a waiter trip up a step. A glob of foam spilled from a cup into one of the saucers on his tray.

'In that case,' I said, returning my gaze to Lizzie, 'what do you think of this guy?'

She threw a look over her shoulder. 'The waiter?'

'*No.*' I scrambled around for my phone. 'This guy.'

Shielding her eyes, Lizzie inspected the phone proffered at her. Her expression sombre, she scrolled down Owen's profile.

'Oh, yeah. Okay,' she said. 'He looks nice.'

'*Nice?* Is that it?'

'What? I thought you wanted a nice guy. Isn't that what we were just talking about?'

'Yeah, but I want someone who's more than nice. They can be nice, but they've got to have a certain …'

'*Je mange tout?*' She paused, looking up at me. '*Je ne sais quoi?*'

'Yeah. Wait, what was the first thing you said?'

'I don't know. I don't speak French.'

'Okay, well, yes, *je ne sais quoi.* Exactly. He's got to have a bit of that.'

She flicked through Owen's photos thoughtfully. 'Look, I'm not sure what you want me to say. I don't know if he has the *je ne sais quoi,* but he definitely looks … odd.'

'Odd?' I baulked. But, oh, it was useless to pretend I didn't see it as well. In one of his pictures, Owen was sitting in a wheelbarrow full of mannequin arms.

'But he seems funny, no? Interesting?' I suggested.

'Oh yeah, definitely interesting,' Lizzie nodded furiously, sensing my desperation. 'And definitely not the kind of guy you usually go for. No way is he a fuckboy. Or a softboy, whatever that is.'

Taking my phone from her, I leaned back in my chair and wiggled my sunglasses anxiously.

'Oh, I don't know now,' I grumbled. 'He's asked me out next Friday and I don't know whether to go. I don't know if he's my type, looks-wise.'

'Well, who cares about that?' Lizzie shrugged. 'You were just saying that the fit ones are living in gargantuan oysters.'

'Alright, fine,' I heaved. 'But more importantly, what if he's another loon? I don't know if I can handle another one, Lizzie.'

'You'll never know if you don't go,' she enthused. 'Nothing ventured, nothing gained. You might have a great time. Then again ...' She trailed off, suddenly distant. 'Well,' Lizzie said pointedly, 'I don't have the best track record with weird guys. So maybe you should ignore me.'

Our eyes met, and I chortled into my iced latte. She wasn't wrong. Lizzie had had way more than her fair share of strange men. A few months ago she'd told a 'nice, eccentric' guy that she wanted to keep things casual, and he responded by intermittently texting her: *Hey, how are you?* then blocking her before she had the chance to respond. In his mind, this was probably a power move.

She'd given another eccentric a go weeks later, but politely called it quits after the third date. He responded by calling her multiple times and, when she didn't pick up, began detailing his day, in minutiae, for a month. The final message read: *Hey Lizzie! I thought of you today. My dad and I are starting work on a pirate galleon chocolate cake. I made a sailing-themed playlist to put on while we bake. I thought this would be the sort of thing you would like.*

'Is it?' I asked her.

'No,' she said.

So should I have taken Lizzie's advice on seeing this potentially mad man? Probably not. But would I? Well, I *did* have a free Friday. And maybe things with Owen would be a little different, I thought. He wasn't anything like the guys I'd previously dated. Maybe I'd have the upper hand this time (or at least not the lower one).

Plus, as she noted, nothing ventured, nothing gained ...

As much as I'd banged on about Owen's appearance, I was more preoccupied with my own the day I went to meet him. The pre-period hormones were in full swing, and I had the premenstrual skin to match. Compact in hand, I dabbed foundation over my already-caked face and grimaced. Here's hoping he liked my personality.

Hypocritically, a bald patch at the back of Owen's head was the first thing I noticed about him. But then he turned, and I was met by a pair of very blue eyes.

'Hello!' he said nervously, holding open the door of the bar we'd agreed to meet at.

'Hi.' With a small smile in return, I bowed my head and stepped inside.

Lifting it back up, I was hit by a wall of déjà vu. Months after disgracing myself with Joel, here I was again – back at the Little Bat.

Owen and I settled on two plush chairs by the window. 'Shall we share a bottle?' he asked, a twinkle in his eye.

'Sure,' I agreed, setting down my menu with vigour. 'Why not?'

Bolstered by this response, Owen sprang up and sauntered over to the bar. I only really took stock of his outfit when I watched him return. Full of unconventional choices, he wore a black, Western-style shirt, skinny jeans and sneakers. With the bottle in his right hand, I noticed that every finger wore a ring.

Lo and behold, this peculiar style had a personality to match.

What surprised me was that I didn't mind – not at all. Owen wasn't strange in the same threatening way Jack was. Yes, he was jocular and provocative, but with the familiarity of an old friend. He howled with laughter when I gave him a comedic spin on my dating history. And with every one of my lame jokes, he cracked a wry smile and called me a nerd.

'Anyway, I'm going to stop talking about all that,' I chuckled, half an hour in. Scooting back in my chair, I looked at him carefully. 'So, what about you?' I asked. 'Where do you work? What's been your worst date?'

He worked with robots. 'AI, etc.' And she'd arrived in a frothy yellow dress, begged to come home with him, and had finished the night by giving him 'the saddest blow job ever'.

'What does that mean?' I was genuinely curious.

'Er.' He shifted in his chair, running a thumb over his smile. 'Well, she didn't seem very happy to be doing it. But when I told her that she didn't have to and that she could stop, she'd just … go at it harder.'

'Fucking hell. That's a bit odd.' I sipped my drink. 'And too much pressure, I would have thought.'

'*Way* too much pressure,' he nodded.

Owen went on to reveal that he (supposedly) knew Nick Cave, (definitely) had a psychedelic funk band (I looked them up), and owned a van with a bed in it. I blinked. Did he live in the van?

'No,' he laughed, leaning back and lifting the toes of his shoes. 'I own an actual flat with an actual garden, I'll have you know. Look, I'm even growing tomatoes.' Reaching into his pocket, Owen pulled out his phone and showed me a picture, practically beaming with pride.

'Wow! Green thumbs and all.' I smiled up at him, registering for the first time that I was quite tipsy.

'Ha. Yeah.' With a nod, Owen slipped his phone back into his pocket. 'We can grow some if we ever live together,' he added breezily.

I spluttered slightly on my wine. Fucking hell, had this guy just mentioned living together? On the first date? Was he trying to freak me out? Lowering my glass, I decided to brush this rather intense comment under the rug. Maybe he'd said it without thinking, I thought.

An hour later, Owen began massaging his lower back.

'Do you mind if we move over to the sofa?' he asked, his face wrinkling. 'These chairs are a bit – ah – uncomfortable.'

'Yeah, sure.' As long as we're just moving over there and not into a home together, I wanted to add.

I tried to mask my surprise when he chose the exact spot Joel and I had been entwined in, months before. It was either serendipity or a very bad sign.

Owen refilled our glasses with the last of the bottle, then ordered another. Soon enough, we were laughing almost constantly. His leg started brushing against mine, his hands reaching across the table. And just when the room started to look lopsided, he took hold of my chin and kissed me.

I was shocked by how good it was. Owen was a masterful kisser, giving me just enough and then pulling away at the pivotal moment. He would come back soft, touching the tip of my tongue, then he'd go in deep. It was amazing.

Reaching a fever pitch, Owen's fingers trailed up the back of my neck and I gasped.

'Oh my God,' he breathed into my ear. His breath was hot against my cool skin, and though our bodies were pressed against each other, he endeavoured to pull me closer. I moaned slightly – yes, in the middle of a bar, I *know*, but I couldn't help it. The air around us was swimming with electricity.

After a few more minutes of kissing, he pulled away and said: 'Fuck. I'm having a hard time not carrying you out of here, Kitty.'

I nodded, feeling slightly faint. 'Shall we get the bill?'

Before I'd finished the sentence Owen had his hands in the air, writing an imaginary cheque. I was relieved to see a different waiter to last time arrive with the card machine.

We left shortly afterwards. And then, in the middle of the silent street, Owen hoisted me up so that I was straddling him. Pushing my hair aside, I lowered my face to kiss his.

'God, I'm glad I've met you,' Owen breathed into the humid air. I smiled as he put me back down, saying nothing.

Our PDA continued when we said goodbye at the station. '*My* man! I've got mad respect for you,' a passer-by shouted at Owen. 'You is going *in*.'

Snickering, we broke apart. I felt my face redden, suddenly aware of how gross we were being.

'We should probably stop,' I said, lowering myself onto the flats of my feet. 'We're putting people off their kebabs.'

'Yeah, alright,' Owen chuckled, his eyes twinkling again. 'Only … we don't have to do it here. We could go back to mine, if you like.'

And oh, I was tempted. If he was this good at kissing, imagine how amazing he'd be in the bedroom, I thought breathlessly. But no: tonight was not the night. I was firm about that, after Leo. Best not to let this thing peak too early, only to leave me high and dry.

'I have a free flat next weekend, though,' I added furtively.

'Next weekend? Next weekend is perfect.' Looking down at me, Owen's tender expression split into a grin.

I was smiling too as I sank down on the tube home. Well, Lizzie had been right, I thought with a refreshing swell of optimism. Nothing ventured, nothing gained. I was so glad I'd gone.

It was 7pm when I went to meet Owen the following Saturday, and still luxuriously hot. I wriggled my dress down my thighs as I walked, glancing down at it with a smile. It was my favourite dress that summer: fitted and strappy and covered in lemons.

Owen looked shy when I waved at him, pulling me in as soon as he could. I didn't even notice the bald patch this time.

'Hello,' he murmured into my freshly washed hair. 'Good to see you.'

'You too,' I mumbled into his shirt. Pausing for a moment, I breathed in the aftershave hanging on it and closed my eyes. Mm, this was nice.

'Well,' I smiled eventually, pulling away. 'Shall we go inside?'

Apparently still shy, Owen nodded.

I watched him fidget with his rings as we looked around for a free table inside the pub, and wondered why he was suddenly so nervous. Taking in his rigid body, I felt his nerves transmit to mine, though I'd felt calm and secure on the walk to meet him. As we sat down on a low, leather sofa, I found myself sitting far away, awkwardly perching by one of its arms.

'What are you doing over there, you weirdo?' Owen laughed, patting the space beside him.

I laughed as well, shuffling closer. 'Sorry,' I said, pinkening. 'I'm just a bit nervous.'

'Well, don't be,' Owen smiled, squeezing my shoulder. His voice was soft, genuine. Reassuring.

'Aren't you nervous?' I asked, looking at him. My own nerves seemed to have chased his away.

'I *was*,' he confirmed. 'But you've calmed me down by reminding me what a massive nerd you are.'

'Oh, wow. Thanks.'

Owen chuckled. 'No, it's just …' He paused, lowering his eyes. 'Well, I hoped I would fancy you as much as last time, and when I saw you I was like "wow" – I actually fancy you even more.'

'Oh.' I gave him a small smile. 'That's sweet.'

'And I just thought, why is this girl with *me*? But, well, I know now.'

I pulled a face. 'Alright. Well, I don't know whether to take that speech as a compliment or an insult.'

'Maybe a bit of both?' Owen grinned. Then he leaned forward and kissed me. It was just as amazing as it was before. 'And now that I've pulled myself together,' he resumed, sliding away, 'what would you like to drink?'

Two gin and tonics later, we were having just as much fun as last time – maybe even more. His bohemian lifestyle, bizarre band and bonkers neighbours made for some hilarious stories, and though mine were a lot more banal, he drank them in. We could have been two best friends, the way we were talking, except Owen kept stopping to kiss me.

And the more tipsy he became, the more ardent his adulation. It crept into our easy, jocular conversation and caught me off guard.

'I could stare at you for hours,' he told me at one point, holding my face in his hands.

I stared back at him, mesmerised. Not by his face, necessarily, but by his intensity. It was strange and intoxicating – a smoke filling my lungs and making me giddy. I looked into his eyes, full of reverence, and quietly said thank you.

'I just can't believe you're here with me,' he went on. 'When I saw you earlier, I really did wonder what the hell you were thinking, coming tonight.'

'Well, thanks,' I smiled again.

As affirming as it was, it did become a little too much, after a while. By the end of the date, his self-flagellation was starting to make me feel awkward. There were only so many times I could say 'thank you'; only so many times I could protest against his self-effacing comments. All the same, there was something addictive about his adoration. I filed his compliments away in my mind, feeling drunk with power. And, as the evening wore on, just drunk. So drunk that I barely remember how we got back to my flat, but suddenly there we were. Getting undressed.

Owen towered over me on the bed – skin flushed, brow knitted.

'You're so sexy,' he murmured, kissing my breasts. 'And I don't know … well, I don't know if you think *I'm* sexy, but …'

Oh God. I rolled my eyes, glad he couldn't see my face. Less of the self-flagellation, please! I wanted to say. This was all getting a bit needy. Surely he didn't want me to keep arguing with him; to insist how sexy he was? In the end, I simply told him to stop being silly, but the silliness had just begun.

After frenziedly ripping my pants off, Owen plunged inside and remained there for a whole ten seconds before it was over. When he pulled himself back out, his face was a deep shade of burgundy.

'I am *so, so* sorry,' he told me in a shuddering whisper, as if he'd run over my cat.

Awkwardly, I sat up and pulled my knees to my chest, attempting a reassuring smile.

'Don't worry, it happens,' I told him, my voice strangely high. Mute, he shook his head, pulling the condom off with a 'thwack' and dropping it into the bin. A few long, drawn-out moments passed.

'Honestly, don't worry,' I bleated.

Owen didn't respond, so I gave up and shuffled to the end of the bed. 'Er, I'll be back. Just nipping to the loo.' There was no way I was going to get a UTI after ten seconds of dissatisfying sex, I thought. No way.

When I returned, Owen was making the bed.

'It's the least I can do,' he lamented, shamefaced. Looking at me doubtfully, he added: 'Would you like me to leave?'

I didn't want to embarrass him further, but couldn't help but laugh.

'Will you stop making such a big deal about this?' Sitting down on the bed, I forced Owen to look at me, taking his red face in my hands. 'It happens to loads of people. *Loads.* It's fine.'

He nodded sadly in response, and we crawled under the covers.

In the wee hours of the morning, Owen redeemed himself (and then some), to both of our delight. At 5 a.m. we lay together smiling, my head on his chest, early summer light trickling in through the curtains.

He hung around the next day – using my shower; kissing me in the hallway and in the kitchen. Then he left around lunchtime, messaging me twenty minutes later.

Towel drying my hair, I looked down at my phone with vague surprise.

Miss you already! xx Owen said. Kiss kiss.

It was a relief, not having to wait in a mist of anxiety for the first post-sex text. Not having to bat away the fearful thoughts of having been a bad lay. But it also made me a little, just a *little*, uneasy. I liked Owen, but still wasn't in the market for a boyfriend. And even if I suddenly decided that I was, I didn't see myself falling in love with him.

Not that I thought he was in love with me either, but he seemed like a pretty intense guy. A guy who was already invested. What if he wanted to text every hour of every day? I asked myself with apprehension.

I was right to worry about this. As it happened, Owen *did* want to message every hour of every day. And if that wasn't full-on enough, he'd reply in a matter of seconds.

Why don't you have your read receipts on? he asked me after a two-hour interim.

I do, don't I? I replied, perfectly aware that I'd switched that function off. So that you don't hassle me, I wanted to retort.

You should turn them on., Owen said. Full stop, no kiss.

On Sunday, he told me that remembering our night had made him unsuitably hard in public, and that he needed to see me ASAP. He sent a long, winding voice memo and requested one back. Then he sent me a picture of where he was sitting in the park. I stared down at my phone and bit my lip, beginning to feel claustrophobic.

And yet some of the headiness from our dates was still hanging about. It filled my bedroom, puffing me up when I felt deflated; buoying me when I felt my insecurities pulling me under. I wanted to keep his compliments in my mind, tight and secure like a precious message in a bottle. Though I could tell he wasn't right for me and that our fling would probably end in tears, I wasn't ready to let go of the way he made me feel.

It's odd to look back on this state of mind. I wonder why I needed validation from a stranger like Owen, someone who had only known me for a few days. At this point in 2019, I'd become addicted to compliments from men, and felt inadequate without their fawning. Leo was partly to blame for this. He'd given me a deliciously big ego boost – if a man so beautiful said that *I* was beautiful, surely it had to be true, I thought at the time. Then his disappearing act threw this compliment into doubt. If I was really so great and attractive, why did he stand me up then go quiet for weeks? I was forever playing catch-up after that, trying to prove that his depiction of me was at least a *little* bit accurate. That his compliments hadn't been lies to get me into bed. I'd never been ghosted post-sex before, and it had done a number on my confidence. Suddenly I was desperate to prove that I was attractive enough to hold a man's attention; that I wouldn't be ghosted again and again. The prospect terrified me.

In addition to feeling rejected by Leo, I was also reeling from Conor's rape. I wasn't conscious of it at the time, but his rape had left me feeling far more worthless than I'd ever felt before. *You let that happen to you, to your body,* a small, acerbic voice told me. *In fact, you probably invited it.* Subconsciously, it was proof that I might not be worth kindness and affection and care; that I'd only receive violence in the bedroom. I didn't want that to be true, and then along came Owen, who treated me like some kind of goddess. How could I push him away?

Two days later, he messaged to say that he'd cleared his evening just for me. Could I go and meet him?

I had plenty of doubts, but tried not to overthink it. The first two dates had been fun, hadn't they? They could carry on being fun, couldn't they? And nothing ventured, nothing gained …

I told Owen I could go.

I began to regret my decision almost as soon as I saw him. Waiting on a hot pavement outside Kings Cross, I faltered when Owen rounded the corner. White as a sheet, he floated towards me like some sort of malevolent spirit. His smile was hesitant, his hug limp. When I pulled away and looked up at his face, I noticed that he looked … ill. What on earth had happened? And why had he pressed me to meet him?

'You okay?' I asked him, trying to mask my surprise.

'Me? Oh, yes … yes …'

Owen looked out at the traffic as we walked, squinting in the sunshine.

'You just don't seem …' I floundered, completely thrown off by his new attitude. 'Er, you don't seem yourself?'

Passing a hand over his forehead, Owen sighed.

'No,' he said, avoiding my gaze. 'I suppose I'm not. I didn't sleep at all last night.'

'At all? Oh. I'm sorry to hear that.'

I looked down at our shoes.

'Yeah, well,' he muttered, 'the pub's just around the corner.'

As we waited for the traffic lights to change, I thought about how similar this date was to my final one with Jack. This guy, once so thrilled to share every moment he had with me, suddenly wanted to go home. So why had he dragged me out?

Owen didn't perk up with a pint. Rotating the glass with his fingertips, he stared into its depths blankly.

Someone started playing something jaunty on the piano inside the pub, and he glanced upwards. 'I love this song,' he said under his breath, still averting his gaze. These were the first words he'd said in a number of very long minutes. Rotating my own glass, I looked down at our hands, puzzled. Overnight, Owen had become some kind of mopey, vampiric goth. Was it something I'd said? Was it what I was wearing? Was it my hair? Why was he suddenly so removed, so uninterested?

Time and again, I tried to strike up a conversation. *Any* conversation. Every attempt fell flat until I mentioned my friend's wedding next month, then his eyes popped open.

'I don't believe in marriage,' he interrupted, looking at me as if he wanted to make that fact very, very clear. 'In fact, I'm never going to get married. I don't want children, either.'

I gawked at Owen, speechless. Was I wearing a white gown and train? Had I forgotten that I was brandishing a book of baby names? If not, why was he acting like I was desperate to wed him and bear his children? I hadn't even been sure that I wanted to *sleep* with him again. He was the one who had mentioned living together on our first date. Bristling and confused, I sipped my beer.

An hour later, Owen said he felt tired and needed to go home. He didn't kiss me when we parted ways, and I blinked back tears as I boarded the tube.

All of a sudden, my power over him had evaporated, vanishing into the balmy night. I felt bewildered. Crestfallen.

He didn't message twenty minutes after our drinks, or even that evening. The next morning, however, I received this message:

Hey Kitty, sorry I was so weird yesterday. If I'm honest, I'm not really in the best place at the moment. I think something more than casual is a bit much for me. But I don't know. x

What the actual fuck … I grimaced.

Okay. Thanks for letting me know, my thumbs typed. *No pressure. I'm happy to keep things casual, or we could just park it here.*

I felt like I'd been punched in the gut, and by a guy I wasn't even that keen on. Setting my phone down on my desk, I wondered why I was leaving the window open at all. I suppose a part of me wanted to prove that I could regain that intoxicating power over him. To prove that I was worthy of re-experiencing that giddy rush of confidence.

This prospect soon lost its shine, however.

Three days later, Owen messaged asking how my weekend had been. Out at a day festival, I didn't see the message until that evening, along with a follow-up.

Cold shoulder? he demanded.

No, I replied, my insides squirming. *Just out with friends.*

Sinking into the sofa, I tossed my phone aside and inspected the sunburn on my arms. Seconds later, however, I returned to it. Re-reading his message, I began to feel queasy. All of a sudden, Owen was the one in control. I felt vulnerable and exposed; backed into a corner.

Okay, good, he said, moments later. He asked if I was free that night.

I scoffed, taking my bag out of my lap and swinging my legs onto the seat.

Afraid not, I returned. *The sun's knocked it out of me.*

Which wasn't a lie, exactly. But I wouldn't have seen Owen even if I was as bright and fresh as a daisy. The power I held over him was long gone. It was all in his hands now, and you know what? He was giving me the creeps.

Unperturbed, Owen tried again two days later.

Wuu2? he asked (which was very MSN of him), adding: *If you find yourself at a loose end later, let's catch up. I miss you.*

'Oh, go away,' I muttered from the top deck of the bus, firing off a quick response. I was busy, I said. Sorry. And I was busy the next time he asked as well.

Too polite to ghost, Owen and I carried on talking between these booty calls. Soon enough, however, we reverted to being strangers – wriggling to escape a conversation turned dry. Making promises we had no intention of keeping. Feigning an interest which had long since vanished.

Finally, it paled to silence. I told my friends and there was a collective sigh of relief.

'Thank God,' Maisie said, dipping a custard cream into her tea at work. 'He was a fucking weirdo.'

As relieved as I was, I was baffled, too. How had something so hot soured so fast? How had a person who once made me feel so confident pulled the rug out from under me? *Again*? Men kept doing this to me. How did they keep doing this to me?

'Oh, I'm sorry,' Lizzie lamented down the phone. 'I told you you shouldn't listen to me. My crazy radar is way off.'

'Yeah, it's all your fault.'

'Well, don't make me feel bad!'

'No, no. I'm kidding.' I laughed, shaking my head. Walking over to the living room window, I peered past the blossom tree at the street below. It was raining, finally – delicate drops tumbling down through the leaves. 'It's actually been kind of interesting, you know.'

'Interesting? How?'

'Well, I feel like it's taught me *something* about relation-ships,' I said. Pausing, I watched a one-legged pigeon hop out of a gutter and quiver down the street.

'What, like, don't have them with lunatics?'

I rolled my eyes. 'Yeah, that. Also: I don't think I *ever* actu-ally had any power over Owen.'

'No?'

'No. I think him giving me power was a way to actually give *him* power.'

'Oh?' I could hear her switching the kettle on. 'Go on.'

'Well, he built me up only to pull me down, you know? He was paying me all these compliments just so he could mess me about. Oh God, I'm doing that song.'

Lizzie chuckled. After a brief interlude of 'Build Me Up Buttercup', she said: 'So, what, it was like, a control thing?'

'Exactly. He gave me the illusion of control but actually *he* was the one telling me when I should and shouldn't message him. He was the one coming on too strong, before turning it round on me to make it look like I was.'

'Huh.'

'And I read this thing online.' I stopped, running a finger along the windowsill and grimacing at how dirty it was. 'Er, it was about something called "love-bombing". Apparently, people do this stuff all the time. It's, like, this problematic thing you need to look out for when dating. So I've decided to be very wary of ridiculous compliments and tributes, you know? Best case scenario: they're not real. Worst case scenario, they're dehumanising.'

And more often than not, you're only put on the pedestal to be knocked back off again, I concluded to myself. It was better to be on solid ground.

After a brief silence, I heard a sigh crackle down the line.

'Fuckboys, now love-bombing,' Lizzie mumbled. 'I can't keep up.'

———————◆———————

The more I thought about love-bombing, the more I identified it in some of the relationships I'd observed over the years. Friends' boyfriends who worshipped the ground they walked on, only to turn cold and distant before coming back twice as devoted. Those pointless, endless relationships which stopped and started; stopped and started, like a useless, flashy old sports car chugging up a hill. The interminable arguments and reconciliations. The confusion and tears and ultimately sullen silence.

Is that all romance is, then? I asked myself after Owen. Should dating really feel like this? Like a constant grappling for the reins, a breathless power grab? Are we all just insecure people trying to one-up each other? On some level, I was definitely using sex with Owen to prove to myself that I was desirable. I was definitely trying to reclaim the confidence I felt before Leo's rejection and Conor's rape. For many of us, sex promises to patch up our bruised egos, to undo our past traumas, but I've never found this to be true.

I'd hoped that casual sex would be this collaborative, mutually fulfilling thing: a win for both parties. But I kept feeling blindsided, messed around, confused. I'd thought, looking at Owen's profile, that he'd lend me a sense of power. And while he did for a time, it was so short-lived. Ultimately, I had to sit and watch the tables turn yet again.

And if dating was this strange sort of game, why was I so bad at it?

I didn't know, but I knew that I had to change tack.

CHAPTER 6

James

'Hottest on record', 'hottest on record'. Those three words were plastered across every front page in July 2019, the paper curling in on itself in agreement.

It seemed that every Londoner was outside, pounding the dusty pavement with fading trainers or long-neglected sandals. Those in their twenties looked around with keen, hesitant smiles, blinking in the sun and thinking about sex. I was one of those people, hoiking down my lemon-patterned dress as I left the house for yet another date.

I had high hopes for this one. After a brief, post-Owen breather, I was ready to put myself out there again. A little world-weary, but ever hopeful that I could forge a sexual relationship with someone who left me feeling satisfied and whole. For the first time, I was even open to the prospect of love, too. My no-strings flings had had their (occasionally) good moments, but they'd also made me realise how important affection was, too. Well, affection and respect. I liked the idea of having sex with someone who cared about me; someone who had regard for my feelings and treated me as a person, rather than a means to an end.

And would falling in love be so bad? I'd been around the block a few times now – did I have to keep going round and round forever? Especially given the way this year was going, I sighed to myself. Maybe I'd focused too much on casual sex. Perhaps sex within a relationship would leave me feeling more satisfied, more empowered.

Well, I had to try *something* different. Owen and Leo and Conor and Jack and Joel … they'd exhausted me. Perhaps something longer lasting would make me feel less used. More in control. Less disposable. Yes, I wanted to *mean* something to someone.

It was with this frame of mind that I blitzed through matches on Tinder and Hinge. I had a few prospects, but James was by far the best. He was almost ethereally beautiful: all dark waves, brown eyes, full lips and perfect symmetry. I could hardly believe it when he asked me out.

Queasy with nerves, I wobbled across West London's cobbles and slipped into a cosy, upmarket pub. It took a moment for my eyes to adjust to the darkness, then I registered rich old men in tweed as far as the eye could see. Rich old man, rich old man, *another* rich old man, and – there. Hunched over a cider in the corner was the slender frame of my date.

'Hello!' I said, jarringly bubbly. God, I was nervous.

James lifted his dark eyes to meet mine and smiled hesitantly.

'Hello,' he replied in a monotone.

Oh.

Lowering onto a stool, I wondered if he was always so taciturn. If so, this date would be a waste of a precious Thursday evening. Damn it, I knew he was too good to be true.

To my dismay, James' energy continued at a low ebb for the next two hours. In fairness, he did ask me plenty of questions and took genuine interest in what I had to say. But he was so gloomy, so downbeat. Cracking a smile out of him was like cracking open a beer at the end of a long day: satisfying but long overdue.

Just when I decided to cut my losses and go home, however, James suggested that we go to a gig in East London.

'Right now?' I baulked.

'Right now,' he said flatly, as if an impromptu gig on the first date was entirely normal.

I shifted on my stool and considered it. James had been nothing but a human raincloud for the past two hours, his mouth sullen, eyes downcast. He'd been a little standoffish in our texts leading up to the night, but I'd assumed that was an attempt at seeming cool and aloof rather than as a sign of a genuine lack of interest. Up until this point in the evening, I'd decided that it was definitely the latter; that he didn't want to be on the date. I thought he was as keen as I was to climb into an Uber and head home.

But now he wanted to travel across town with me? To pay for two tickets to see a band? Intrigued, however, I agreed.

When our tube heading east arrived, I began to wonder if saying 'yes' had been a mistake. Riding a noisy train was awkward enough with people you did know, let alone with people you didn't.

Full of foreboding, I followed James aboard. Urgh. It was crammed full of perspiring bodies: businessmen with loose ties holding onto the handrails overhead, tourists awkwardly clutching their cameras to their chests. But as we stepped into their midst, I came to a surprising revelation. Pressed up against James like this, chest-to-chest, in this heaving, airless carriage … it was kind of … sexy? And with so many people mute, I realised that we didn't need to speak. It was as if the whole carriage had agreed to a happy pact of silence.

I spent the journey luxuriating in the feeling of James' linen shirt against my bare collarbones, in glancing up at his face and registering, in this close proximity, how truly symmetrical it was. I looked at his brooding gaze, averted, and felt heat prickle up the back of my neck. Good grief, I'd worked myself into a frenzy by the time we arrived at the venue. His moody demeanour was still a little confusing, but the attraction between us was now palpable. It crackled between us when he touched my lower back or passed me a drink.

An hour later, we watched the band come on. Coolly, James suggested that we stand by the bar to avoid the groupies at the front. I nodded, trying to ignore my mounting agitation. *If he doesn't make a move soon, I'll have to beat him to it*, I thought frantically.

And then, when the second song ended, he took my hand. I cut my eyes at him and my heart jumped. Smiling, James tugged the other one gently, turning my body to face his. He looked down at my mouth and—

Wow. Just wow. It was more like a last kiss than a first, his mouth sweetened with cranberry cider. Around us, the air shuddered as the third song drew to a close.

James kept hold of my hand all night. We hung around until the venue shut and then wandered back to the station, only breaking our attachment to pass through the ticket barriers. He boarded the same train I did, rubbing my thumb with his. And when he looked at me, it was with a new expression. Peaceful and happy, as if the clouds had finally parted.

Far, far too soon, it was my stop.

'Well, thanks for a lovely night,' I smiled. James nodded slowly, then bent down to kiss my cheek.

'Text me when you get home?' he asked.

I told him I would, then stepped through the beeping doors.

Ambling down the platform, I waited there for a few moments, lingering to watch the train disappear down the tunnel, a page from a newspaper fluttering after it.

A few days later, I woke up to a stream of messages from James. Late on a Saturday morning, I blinked at text bubbles describing the wedding he'd gone home for.

The cake was a pile of pork pies. I'm not kidding, he said, complete with photographic evidence.

He sent me another photo of the painting he'd commissioned for his parents – their Yorkshire terrier in a monocle and bow tie.

Sliding my phone under the bed covers, I felt something bloom in my chest. James wasn't like anyone I'd met before. He made me feel things I hadn't yet felt. Warmth and a budding, twisting affection; tentative hope tapping on the door. And *he* was so different. His moody demeanour intimated depth and complexity, while the fact that it had thawed – seemingly thanks to me – also suggested kindness and sensitivity. He was a writer, too, and unbelievably gorgeous, with a soft, Sheffield accent. Every box was being tick, tick, ticked.

Could it be that as soon as I'd decided I was ready for love, I'd found it? That *did* seem too good to be true. And, yes, I knew that I was getting way ahead of myself, thinking about love, but I couldn't help but indulge in the excitement. It was exhilarating, intoxicating. Quietly, I let myself bask in it.

I'd never fallen in love before, not really, and I realised how much I wanted to. It was more Charlotte York than Samantha Jones, but all of a sudden I wanted to fall deeply and blindly with no hope of return. I wanted to go to the seaside with someone and spend the night in their room, watching bad TV the next morning. I wanted to wear their T-shirt and read with them, side by side in bed like an old married couple. I wanted to go to their friends' weddings and to their parents' birthday lunches; I wanted to buy thoughtful gifts and to go on double dates. I didn't want to feel discarded anymore; I wanted to feel valued and worthy and adored. In other words, I was finally open to the prospect of a boyfriend. I hoped, somewhere deep down, that James might be my first.

It was with a heavy heart, then, that I met him a second time and found him as glum as he'd been at the start of our first date. Approaching him where he waited beside a Hyde Park gate, misery on his face, I wondered whether I'd painted him in a kinder, more romantic, slightly inaccurate light. In my imagination, he was troubled and complex; in reality he was moody. Was this really his go-to expression? I wondered. And if it was, did I want my first boyfriend to be perpetually dismal? I sighed, sensing another expiration date.

But James surprised me once again. When we sat down with our wine bottle, his face broke into a wide, brilliant smile.

'Shit. Don't suppose you have a corkscrew?' he asked, shielding his eyes from the sun.

I googled how to open the bottle without one, cackling as he tried each 'hack' in turn. I've never met anyone who can pop a cork by slapping it with a shoe, and I don't think I ever will.

Admitting defeat, James retreated to the shop for a replacement. He was still laughing when he returned, plopping down on the grass. New bottle open, we traded anecdotes as the evening crept in overhead. One in particular made me laugh. He and his flatmates had been trying to fill their spare room, and he told me about the host of strange applicants they'd had round.

'So there was one really nice guy. Very chilled, very quiet.'

'Ah, and you went with him?'

'No.' James squinted at two men in the middle distance, his eyes following their Frisbee. 'He didn't leave after seeing the room.'

'Eh? What do you mean?'

'Well, we were in the living room watching *Peep Show*, and he just came in and joined us. He sat down and watched the entire episode, commenting the whole way through.'

I snorted, taking a swig of wine.

'Then he goes: "Let's watch another episode". So we all sit through another one, in silence, until he leaves half an hour later.'

'Bloody hell.' I shook my head. 'People are weird.'

'Yeah. Then there was this other guy who seemed like a great fit, until he told us he had a snake.'

'Ew.' I shuddered. 'That's a hard no.'

'Well, it was the mice, mainly. Imagine having a freezer full of mice.'

I grinned.

'Reaching over them for the Magnums? Yikes.'

James chuckled. His initial gloom had completely lifted, and he looked down at me warmly – the hair on his arm tickling mine. When it was dark, he glanced over at the bottle with the splintered cork and said: 'You know, I've got a corkscrew at home.' I didn't need telling twice.

James took my hand as we stood, holding it between us on the train. My head on his shoulder, we alternated between stories which made us laugh and comfortable silence, looking out at the flickering skyline.

His flat was empty when we arrived. I unzipped my boots and left them by the door, pulling my feet underneath me as I sat down on the sofa. When the second bottle was drained, James climbed on top of me, kissing me first on the mouth and then in a fluttering trail down my arms, stomach and legs.

When he returned to my mouth, his kiss was deeper, more feverish. I moaned, so ready to do this. So ready to have sex with James.

We fucked on the floor, up against a wall, and (bizarrely) in his flatmate's room as well as his own. (I realised this in the morning when I asked where the terrarium had gone.) He was a little rough, but I didn't mind – not even when it started to hurt, not even when I bled. Having James inside me felt like the full stop at the end of a sentence.

Around 5 a.m., I turned and watched him fall asleep. Morning light had begun to creep in through the blinds, lighting his hand like a beacon. I looked at his long lashes and smooth, caramel skin, and thought he was the most angelic person I'd ever seen. Well, shit, I thought. I was in trouble now.

Hours later, James made me a cup of tea, and we sat cross-legged on the bed opposite one another. Our conversation was gentle, lilting, our voices slightly hoarse from last night's wine.

I was still floating somewhere above London when I left, buoyed by a funny message he sent during my walk home. Smirking, I tried to suppress the cocktail of nerves and excitement bubbling inside. I really didn't want to get my hopes up, but they were somewhere far beyond me, now – winging up into a blue July sky.

———————

I was still faintly delirious when I met my friends for dinner a week later.

'He's a writer,' I told my rapturous audience. 'Very sweet. Very gentlemanly.'

'Oh, she's in luuurve,' Beth cooed, stabbing a dumpling with her chopsticks.

'I'm not!' I protested, reddening. Was I?

And then, the next morning, it struck. Seemingly out of nowhere, a violent wave of depression. I hardly remember my day in the office or walking home. I don't remember what I said to Jen when I walked in crying, only that my legs were shaking.

Fuck. A bad spell of depression hadn't visited me in a while. An episode tended to hit me every few months – the trigger could be big or small, but if it cracked open the door to my repressed emotions just a little bit, they would crash through and flood the whole house. Suddenly, all the sadness and grief that I'd been burying in the months since I'd been raped by Conor broke free from the soil. Here came the black fog, covering everything in sight. The anguish was overwhelming. And with a desperate pang of sadness, I watched all of my recent happiness break free from my hands.

It was as if my brain was short-circuiting. But I knew the drill by now: shut yourself away and try not to kill yourself. I threw the paracetemol I'd been saving for my period in the bin and didn't look at the knives when I went into the kitchen, shielding either side of my face with my hands. I just have to get through the next two days, I repeated to myself.

Jen asked me to check in from my bedroom every hour, leaving food outside the door. As I stared at the wall, the static eventually became a low, persistent hum.

And then, two days later, I woke up feeling better. Lighter. Still a little hazy, I unlocked my phone to see that James had messaged twice in my absence, and felt a twinge of guilt. In the thick of this terrible episode, he was a shaft of light encouraging me to feel anything close to hope. Hope that life was worth all these oppresive feelings.

He messaged again on my way into work, asking if I wanted to meet on Friday. I smiled down at the words, wiping them with my sleeve, rain thudding against my umbrella. 'Sounds good,' I replied.

I wasn't sure if I was in a fit state to socialise with anyone this week, but I was keen to see him. It would be a nice distraction, at least.

———————

Unfortunately, history repeated itself.

James arrived at the gig with a stony expression, and yet again my heart sank. *Again* he'd reverted to the first date version of himself: churlish and withdrawn, and I couldn't stomach it in my current state of mind. Fumbling with my bag strap, I stared ahead at another band I didn't care about – lonelier than ever.

The first two hours passed painfully. He wasn't talkative, and I was hardly in the mood to carry a conversation. I was also so frazzled that I frequently misunderstood what he was saying, which frustrated him and dismayed me. But then we stepped outside, and another man said I was beautiful. Oddly, it broke the ice.

'What's a man got to do to get some respect around here?' James grinned, lighting a cigarette.

And just as it had those other times, the gloom suddenly passed. He began regaling me with stories, our backs against the wall to avoid the drizzle.

'Once, I was working in a shop and thought a girl was hitting on me,' he said, smoke billowing out into the humid air. 'She asked for my number, started texting me, and we arranged to meet. Turns out, she'd asked for my number for a friend. I expected Daisy, I got Dick.'

I chortled, rubbing my arms for warmth.

'What did you do?'

'Nothing. We just went and watched the movie anyway. Then I left.'

Chuckling, James dropped his cigarette and stamped it into the pavement, pulling me under his arm. Watching the rain, he told me about the school friends he'd stayed in touch with. Work anecdotes. He didn't ask me many questions, but tonight I didn't mind.

An hour later, we left the bar.

We meandered down a cobbled mews on our way to the station. And then, underneath a wrought-iron street lamp, James kissed me. It was a perfect kiss: tender and affectionate and blissfully romantic. I leaned on his shoulder on the train home, catching our reflection as we pulled into Westbourne Park, our faces ghostly white. He saw it too and kissed the crown of my head.

Oh, I had needed this so much. This gentle, wordless romance; this restorative touch. Maybe he really would become my boyfriend, I thought. Maybe he'd be there to support me if the flashbacks to Conor returned. I knew I shouldn't be clinging to someone as fickle and unknowable as a man I'd only been out with three times, and yet here he was: a symbol of hope. A repository for all of my longing.

Back at the flat, James dropped my hand so that I could unlock the front door. It was late, so I let us in quietly. Treading softly, I led him down the hallway and into my bedroom, both of us giggling at something he'd said. He closed the door behind us then, and started to undress.

From the mattress, I watched James pull his shirt over his head and felt a twinge of affection. I was dizzy with apprehension, drunk on romance. I couldn't wait to feel his bare legs against mine; to wrap myself in the warmth of his tanned, lean arms. I couldn't wait to have him inside me; to feel that full stop again.

But my desire shifted to misgiving when he looked down at me. Why was he … angry? I asked myself, panic-stricken. What had I done?

There wasn't time for more thought. James seized me by the shoulders and shoved me backwards onto the bed, hard. Ow. Well, okay …

He climbed on top of me and kissed me then, pinning my wrists above my head. At first, it was hot – his brown eyes furiously intense. But it got rougher and rougher, and rapidly began to feel weird. Wrong. Something had changed, but I couldn't put my finger on what.

A minute later, James grabbed my throat, squeezing it as if it was an inanimate object – something in the way. His fingers dug into my arms and shoulders, and I winced.

And then, no more than three minutes in, he pushed my knees apart and pummelled his way in. Fuck, it really hurt this time, I noticed with another wince. He'd only been inside for a few moments when I wanted him to stop. On top of the pain, we hadn't used a condom last time and I'd be damned if I let that happen again. I wasn't going to shell out another £30 on a pill which made me hormonal and spotty, weathering the guilt of my third morning-after pill in a year.

No. I needed him to get out now.

'Wait. Wait a second,' I told him breathlessly. 'Condom.'

To my shock, James didn't stop. I blinked. Hadn't he heard me? Or was he *ignoring* me?

'Condom,' I repeated, clearer this time.

Not only did he silently refuse to stop, James fucked me harder.

Between each shuddering pump, I considered saying it again, but at the last moment bit my tongue. If he ignored me a third time, there would be no doubt in my mind that it was deliberate, and I wanted to cling onto that doubt. To deny that this, *this* was actually happening. To pretend that I had the power to make it stop.

And the sooner I let it happen, the sooner it would be over.

When James was finally finished, I slipped away to the bathroom. The humming was back in my head, noisier than ever. It got louder when I saw the purple fingerprints on my right shoulder. My own white face in the mirror. Blood darkening the toilet water.

I returned to my room for a pair of underwear, stuck in a sanitary pad, and crawled back into bed.

'Started my period,' I whispered to James. He put his arms around me.

'Oh. Not ideal,' he muttered, already half asleep.

I lay awake for hours, staring at the same wall I'd bored my eyes into, days ago. I felt cold, suddenly. Stiff and wooden. Like a mannequin.

James was brusque the next morning. Bristling.

He watched me sit on the bed and apply my makeup for a few minutes, then retrieved his jacket from the floor. His goodbye kiss was quick. Forgettable.

I was a perfect Pollyanna until I heard the door close behind him, and then I sat on the floor and cried.

Tears prickled again when I sat down at my work desk later that day.

'How was it?' my colleague Elle asked with relish, whizzing round in her swivel chair.

'I don't know,' I told her honestly.

'What do you mean?' Her eyes widened. 'Are you okay?'

'Yeah, yeah. I think so.' I shook my head, passing a hand through my hair. 'Sorry,' I said. 'I don't know why I'm being so emotional.'

Wheeling her chair over, Elle looked at me with concern.

'You don't seem okay. What happened?' she asked quietly.

'Well, it *was* fine. But I suppose …' I paused, crossing a hand over my chest. 'I suppose it was quite rough. He's, er, left all these bruises.'

For some reason, I said this with a strained chuckle.

'Oh, God.' Elle grimaced, looking at me hard. 'I don't like that.'

Neither do I, I thought. We looked at each other for a moment, then both of us glanced up. Someone was calling us into a meeting.

I stared into space throughout the whole thing, trying to quell a new wave of nausea. I could only think about the morning-after pill now, and how I'd have to get it on my lunch break. How I should avoid the type I chose in May, even though it was cheap, because I didn't want to spend another day bleeding and panicking and crying on the bus. I'd choose the one I got the last time I'd had unprotected sex with James. That one hadn't given me many side effects.

At 1 p.m. I tipped back a bottle of water, the plastic crinkling in my hand. Then I swallowed the tiny pill I'd just bought – along with the pharmacist's look of judgement.

'Have you had the morning-after pill before?' he had asked from across the counter.

'Yes,' I replied.

'This month?'

'Yes.'

'And when was the night of the incident?'

'Last night.'

Frowning, he'd swept off into the storage room and returned with a small cardboard box.

'How are you paying, cash or card?'

'Card,' I replied.

And that was that. The ordeal was over. But I felt sad. So sad.

All the same, I waited a whole week before washing the pillowcase James had slept on. When I finally did, I sat cross-legged on the carpet, staring into the drum. I stayed there for a few moments, watching it toss and turn in the soapy water.

Our WhatsApp conversation, once so jocular, became strained. Distant. A fortnight after 'the incident', it fizzled to nothing.

Numb, I wrote some lyrics in my notes app: 'Yeah I know the sun's not shining / In fact it sounds a lot like lightning / But if I wake up and we break up, well that's alright by me.' And as the weeks went by, I discovered how wonderfully accurate that was. No longer being with James was absolutely *fine* by me, I discovered. I wasn't nearly as heartbroken as I thought I'd feel.

That song became my friends' favourite, and when I opened my first paid gigs with it, months later, I felt a swell of satisfaction. As they swayed in front of me, singing along, I decided that I'd made something out of that horrible experience. I'd turned James' violence into happiness; into something which made me feel proud. So maybe that made it okay. Maybe that made it worth it.

Except it didn't. Not at all. In reality, though I was fine with never seeing James again, I was far more wounded by my last night with him than I initially believed. I didn't call it rape for many, many months – just 'something that had happened'.

And then, months later, I was scrolling through Instagram when I stumbled on a post from a rape charity. In quotation marks were examples of the lies survivors tell themselves after they've been raped. One of them stood out: 'Maybe he didn't hear me.'

And suddenly it was so, so clear. Of course James had heard me. Of course I had been raped. I dropped my phone on the seat beside me and started crying, covering my face with my hands.

All year I'd spoken to friends about that night, omitting crucial, uncomfortable details. Looking back, I registered that I'd been talking to them like I was trying to crack a code, or piece together a crime scene. (Which is what my bedroom was that night, I thought, feeling slightly sick. And I'd have to go back there every night to sleep.)

For a long time, I just didn't have the language for what had happened to me – I couldn't articulate it, even to myself. I was simultaneously still coming to terms with what happened with Conor, and the weight of the realisation that I may have been raped twice in a year was too unbearable to face for a while. It took years (and eventually some therapy) to come to terms with both events, which were different in detail but painfully similar in the feelings they left me with. It's an ongoing process, actually – I'm still processing those rapes as I write this now. Every now and then, the traumatic memories still knock me backwards. Sometimes they make me snappy or short with the people I love; sometimes I can't make sense of simple tasks because of the flashbacks, and feel overwhelmed and overcome by the slightest inconvenience. Unable to face the men who violated me, my sudden bouts of anger have nowhere to go. Railing against them to friends feels like shouting into the wind, so I push the feelings down and try to forget that they exist.

When my brain was first ready to tell my body it had been raped by two people in a year, I felt an almost unbearable weight of grief. All the bravado of my song fell away. Fear followed me everywhere after I came to that realisation – down the street, telling me that someone was looking at me funny. Into work, telling me that coworkers had ulterior motives. I was so, so afraid it would happen again. Because of course it would – I'd been raped twice in twelve months. Obviously, it would happen again.

I flashbacked to being ten years old on the edge of a field, blinking back tears and shock and shame and bafflement. Asking what the fuck had just happened. How it had happened. Whether I was somehow to blame. I felt powerless and small and strange in my own body; trapped in a person I no longer knew. Everything was odd and off-kilter, as if my thoughts were speaking in another language. I felt alone, completely alone, and very, very scared.

Even worse than the fear was the sadness. Years after that night with James, it still waits at the door whenever I'm in a room alone. It still looks at me through the keen, gentle eyes of birds as they hop across the garden. I breathe it in when I step outside, spring beginning to touch the trees.

I don't know what upsets me the most. James' rape somehow seemed even worse than Conor's. Was it because I was apparently falling in love for the first time? Was it that I once felt so seen and heard by James, as well as held? Was it because I didn't hate him, even now? Even after he'd changed my body and mind forever?

I don't have the answers to those questions, but I still feel sad about that night with James. I think I always will.

And still, somehow, life goes on. Months passed before I listened to the musician he looked like, but eventually I pressed play. The dress James had torn, bundled up at the bottom of my wardrobe, didn't stay there forever. The following summer I dug it out and spread it wide on my bed in the crime scene I'd redecorated, inspecting the ripped zipper between my thumb and forefinger.

Dropping it into my bag, I ferried it to the local dry cleaners and asked if they could do anything about it. They could and, a week later, handed it back to me – almost as good as new. I stopped in a café toilet on the way back and changed into it, just so that I could wear it home.

I'm sorry if that chapter was difficult to read because something similar happened to you. I'm sorry if you were also raped when you felt depressed and anxious. I'm sorry if the assault made your depression and anxiety much, much worse.

Mental health isn't always mentioned in conversations about rape. We harp on the grisly details and statistics and how, in a wider sense, it reflects a dangerous and bleak world for women. Those things are important, yes, but the conversation shouldn't end there. We should ask how the prevalence of rape and sexual assault impacts the emotional wellbeing of so many women. I was mentally fragile when I was raped by James, and if I hadn't had the support of my friends and family and my boss (a woman who gave me the time and space to look after myself), I could have easily sunk into a deep depression to the point of no return. Like I said earlier, to this day I still have moments of feeling uncomfortable in my own skin; my body is still strangely unfamiliar at times. When I'm feeling low, I wonder how I can go on existing in a frame which I no longer seem to own.

It's a deeply unpleasant feeling, and one which I'm not sure I'll ever be able to shake. I'm not saying this for sympathy, but to emphasise how long-lasting the impact of rape is, as you'll know if it's happened to you. The horrors of that trauma don't end the morning after; they trickle into so many areas of your life.

Two years after I was raped, I saw a psychiatrist and was diagnosed with Generalised Anxiety Disorder. I went to see him because I'd been having panic attacks before giving presentations at work, which worsened around the time of Sarah Everard's murder. After the news broke, danger seemed to glare at me everywhere I turned. Women aren't safe in the world, I told myself again and again. The news confirmed that we should be on high alert at all times. Our hearts should always be pounding; our hands closing into quick, uncertain fists.

I started having nightmares which left me stiff and sweaty when I woke up. I shelled out extra money for Ubers instead of walking home at 8 p.m. I'd flash back to Conor and James on top of me.

'It can't happen again. It can't happen again,' I'd tell myself through hot, suffocating tears. 'I can't be raped again.' All of a sudden, I felt like an angry, frantic caged animal, circling my pen and staring outside.

If you've experienced something similar, you'll know how exhausting that feeling is. How it drains you of energy before your day even begins. How it makes you want to stay in bed and curl up into nothing. How it makes you want to forget that you live in a traumatised body; in a traumatised mind.

Know also that you're not alone in that feeling. Not by a long shot.

CHAPTER 7

Freddie

Back in 2019, summer was ending. In a way that felt both gradual and sudden, the world became quiet. Voices lowered, doors closed, and I felt restless. Hurt, too, but unable, at this point, to pinpoint why.

Instead of looking inward, I turned outward, hoping for someone new to distract and excite me. I needed that good first-date high again. I needed to feel desire for someone and that someone desired me. Above all, I needed to forget about James.

So, who would the next person be? I asked the last days of August. It was fairly clear, at this point, that my *Sex and the City* fantasy had completely disintegrated. Samantha Jones I was certainly not, and nor was I Charlotte York. Neither flings nor a (seemingly) serious relationship had given me what I was looking for: fulfilling, empowering sex. But maybe I was partially to blame for this, I surmised. Maybe my taste in men really *had* been awful, as I'd suggested to Lizzie months ago.

Still, there were a few months left in 2019, which meant there was time to turn this horse around. Perhaps my taste in men was better now, I thought with some misgiving. Perhaps I'd be better at choosing someone with lightness and easiness, a kind glint in their eye. What I really wanted right now, I decided, was someone who would make me laugh. Someone who made me forget about the nauseating spin cycle of being a single woman in a capital city. Someone who didn't take more than they gave. Someone who made life feel a little less bleak.

Yes, I concluded. This time, I'd go out and find someone who was funny. Someone who wouldn't use or abuse me or scar me or mess me around. I'd lean again towards a simple, easy, no-strings fling, but with the right person this time. That was the key.

Looking down at Hinge, I decided that Freddie seemed to fit the bill. Not many men can claim Elmo as their wingman but, according to his profile, he was one of them.

I found him while half-drunk on a Tuesday evening, lying upside down in bed, slack-jawed and swiping. I'd found myself going left on almost every profile prior – left after left after left after left. Like so many single women before me, I asked where all the decent people had gone. The ones in front of me had been a sorry bunch: Emmanuel, who said he wanted to suck my blood; Dom, who announced that he could only fall for a girl who 'had, in some way, fallen for herself'. And then a profile named 'A Rest'. The picture was of a medieval knight by a campfire, and the description ran as follows: 'Join me at my campfire, there is mead and mutton. Share your tales and struggles, and I shall listen. Stay as long as you need, traveller.'

Good God. I was quickly losing hope.

And then I saw Freddie, his arm around Elmo. 'Children's TV and radio presenter', his description read. My eyebrows shot up. 'Presenter' implied a certain amount of charisma, while the 'children's' element suggested wholesomeness and a sense of humour, too. He'd be friendly and funny and larger than life, making silly puns out of the corner of his mouth. Yes, this was exactly, *exactly* what I needed.

I couldn't deny that his moderate fame was exciting, too, but it was also non-threatening. It wasn't Orlando Bloom-level intimidating (ha, not by any means), but he wasn't a million miles away from Reggie Yates, either. Maybe I'd get to go to a red carpet, I thought with a flurry of excitement.

Freddie's 'public figure' status appealed for another reason, too. So many of the problems I had with online dating revolved around a lack of accountability. Maybe men treated you poorly because they knew they could get away with it; there were no mutual friends or colleagues who would discover what they'd done, nobody to ask them how things had gone or why they didn't talk to you anymore. Ghost-like in every sense, they existed in a vacuum of irresponsibility.

But if I googled Freddie, everything I wanted to know about him would materialise in front of me. Right there, on the right-hand side of the screen. He was so tangible, so high-profile. Maybe this would make him more accountable and, therefore, less likely to be a dick. Returning to his dating profile, I looked down at his megawatt smile and hit 'match'. Yes, I had a good feeling about Freddie.

As I predicted, our chat on Hinge was amiable and light-hearted. To my delight, the messages made me laugh out loud at work, causing Layla to ask, more than once, what was so funny.

'Nothing,' I said furtively, returning my eyes to my computer. I didn't want to jinx it before we'd even met.

After a week of back-and-forth, Freddie and I finally agreed to go for a drink. He suggested the Soho Theatre Bar, so I slid on some lipstick and took a train to central London. The bar was packed – groups mooching in, searching for chairs, then slinking back out in defeat.

'I'm on a stool,' Freddie told me in a message. 'Hurry up. A beady-eyed woman keeps looking at your seat.'

Huh. Was he? I looked around, but couldn't see Freddie anywhere. Thankfully, he caught my arm before I took a second hopeless turn about the room. We laughed, and I heaved myself onto the barstool opposite. Seeing him now, I wasn't surprised that I'd missed him – with a small pang of disappointment, I found that his photos and description had been a little misleading. For a start: he certainly wasn't six foot two. Secondly, he was a lot more dishevelled in person. His baggy shirt was tired and crumpled, his dark hair stiff with gel.

None of that mattered, though, because Freddie really was funny – even funnier than his messages and job title suggested. Ten minutes into our date, actual tears were streaming down my face. I drank in his stories of eccentric daytime TV hosts and radio presenters he'd met, the story of the *The Apprentice* star who went on about her nudes at media training.

'If you look hard enough, you can still find them,' he mimicked, lifting his pitch and perfecting her accent. 'Honestly, they're out there.'

'God.' I snorted. 'Why are you so good at that voice?'

'The thing is, *nobody* was asking her,' he pressed on, sipping his beer and licking his lips. 'After a while, she latched onto the eighteen-year-old guy doing work experience. "They're out there," she kept saying to him, "just google my name."'

Freddie exchanged more celebrity gossip for another round, and soon we'd sunk enough booze to make the walls spin.

I excused myself to the toilet, fumbling my way to a stall.

'Oh no,' I muttered, giggling as I struggled to find the seat. When I finally sat down, I blinked hard – willing myself sober. But it was too late. Sobriety was long gone.

I returned to the table still giggling, ordering another two cocktails along the way. I knew in the back of my mind that this was a very bad idea, but I couldn't help it. I was having so much fun with Freddie. It was unbelievably refreshing – simply meeting a guy and having a laugh with him. Exchanging anecdotes and trying his drink without any kind of sinister undercurrent. I'd almost forgotten what this was like.

Seemingly, he was having a good time, too.

'I've got to say,' he announced, reaching across the table for my hands, 'I haven't had a date this good for a long time.'

'Neither have I,' I said, smiling. His hands felt nice on top of mine. Big and firm and reassuring.

The next three hours passed like three minutes, partly down to our compatibility – mostly due to the alcohol. We outstayed the theatre-goers first, then our welcome. Finally, we staggered out into the August night, cackling at a joke we'd both forgotten.

I don't remember our first kiss, nor the journey back to his. I had been well and truly laughed into bed, and enjoyed every second of it.

Which was lucky, because – looking back – I wonder if he took advantage, rather, plying me with cocktails and then whisking me home. What makes me feel okay about it is that I still had my bearings. Even though the memories are patchy, I never felt out of control or manhandled in the same way I felt with Conor. It was different.

I'm also not certain he knew how drunk I was. The next morning, Freddie told me that I'd dropped my Caffè Nero loyalty card at the ticket barriers when we reached the underground, and that I'd refused to pick it up.

'It was a point of pride,' he said, shaking his head. 'The ticket man had to let me back through the gates to put it in your purse. You weren't having any of it.'

'God.' I lowered my face into my hands. 'I'm sorry. I was so drunk.'

'Were you?' Freddie asked, and he looked at me with genuine surprise. In the moment I really did believe him – he would have been an Oscar-worthy actor if he was lying.

So anyway, yes: I slid into Freddie's bed the night I met him with complete and total abandon. We kissed each other passionately in the dark, my hands working their way up his back under his T-shirt, his twirling around the hooks on my bra.

Unfortunately, it was then that the mania began to set in. I'm not sure what caused it, exactly – hours and hours of laughing, perhaps, or the seven Cosmopolitans swirling around my system – but suddenly I was hyperactive, exuberant and very, very embarrassing.

As Freddie unclasped my bra, I decided that licking his arms was a very sensual idea. I climbed on top of him and did it with gusto, dragging my increasingly dry tongue from wrist to shoulder.

The sober part of my brain stepped out of my writhing body and yelled: *What are you doing? Stop acting like a lunatic.* But it was no use. The drunk, hysterical part was far more dominant.

Peak embarrassment came after I'd given him a blow job. To this day it's the most embarrassing thing I've ever done.

Worse than falling over in the Year Eight school assembly; worse than when I had a French Connection interview and described my style as 'French'. Worse than pronouncing 'linguine' as 'ling-ween' at an intimidatingly posh restaurant.

And I can't explain why I did it. Was his cum laced with some kind of hallucinogenic? Who knows. I have no way of explaining why I started mumble-warbling Lana Del Rey lyrics to his penis, but that's what I did.

'Shh,' he interrupted, bemused.

Thankfully, I obeyed. Then I looked around for a bin and thought: Oh. I'm going to be sick.

———————

That would have been the cherry on top of the humiliation cake, wouldn't it? But thankfully, I didn't throw up.

This didn't make me feel any better when I woke up at 7 a.m., remembering my straight-to-penis performance with a chill trembling down my spine. No, no, I groaned to myself, sweat gathering on my brow. *Please* say I dreamed that. Did I dream that?

Wincing, I turned my head to look at Freddie, but he wasn't there. I heard a toilet flush and noticed a door on the other side of the room, then quickly turned back to face the wall. I was far too hungover and embarrassed to face him. Maybe if I stayed very still, he'd forget I was here.

Just before closing my eyes, however, I noticed a long, blonde hair on the mattress beside me. It was far too long to be mine, I thought, staring. So he'd had someone else in his bed that recently?

It made me feel a little less ashamed, at least – if I was just one of many women tumbling in and out of this bed, he'd forget all about my serenade. Hopefully. But it also made me feel kind of gross. I didn't like the idea of being another blonde conquest for a D-list celebrity. That was kind of ick.

A couple of hours later I pretended to wake up, sunshine breaking through the blinds.

'Well, that was fun,' Freddie chuckled, grinning at the ceiling.

'It was,' I agreed, my voice distant.

We exchanged ten sentences of croaky chat before I began to hunt for my clothes, scattered around his untidy bedroom. Sliding a pair of sunglasses up my nose with a grimace, I then followed Freddie down the stairs and out of the door.

He told me that he was going to Cardiff later, standing on the threshold in a tight football tee and boxers.

'But I'll text you,' he assured me. Then he kissed me goodbye.

Wandering around the arse end of South London, I groaned when I put my address into Citymapper and discovered that it would take me *80* minutes to get home. Gingerly sinking into my train seat, I closed my weary eyes against the pale morning sun.

───────◆───────

Later that day, I hauled myself onto another train – this time up to Tunbridge Wells, where Lizzie lived. I'd gone to spend the weekend with her in Kent, grey, sweaty, and with a pounding headache. Waving, she pulled up outside the station in her car.

Lifting my bag into the boot, she laughed at the pair beneath my eyes.

'Big night?' Lizzie asked.

'Yes,' I sighed.

I told her about being possessed by the spirit of Lana Del Rey; about how I would never hear from this man again.

'Oh, I'm sure you will.'

Shrugging, I plugged the aux cord into my phone and asked what she wanted to listen to.

'"Video Games"?' Lizzie tittered, clearly proud of herself, giving the steering wheel a little squeeze. 'Sorry. I couldn't resist.'

'You know what? What's even more embarrassing is that it wasn't that obvious,' I complained. Scrunching my eyes against the light of the sky, still too bright, I wondered if leaving the country was an extreme reaction to giving the world's worst blow job.

'What do you mean?' Lizzie chuckled. 'What song did you sing?'

'"Looking for America",' I nearly sobbed.

Lizzie baulked, holding the steering wheel very tightly so that she didn't veer off the road.

'You sang "Looking for America" to his penis?'

'Yes.'

'Oof. Yeah, that's bad.' Lizzie glanced into the rearview mirror, adjusting her glasses. 'I have to say, if someone sang an obscure Lana Del Rey song to my vagina, I probably wouldn't see them again.'

'And I wouldn't blame you.' Sinking back into my chair, I stared at the windshield glumly.

But later that night, the impossible happened: Freddie actually messaged me. I was so surprised I jumped up from the sofa, doing a little jig of triumph.

Back on the lash, his message told me. There was a picture of a murky pint attached. *How's your weekend going?*

'Well, there you go,' Lizzie said, moving the bowl of popcorn away from my knees. 'I told you he'd message. And the next day, too. That's good.'

'I can't believe it,' I sighed proudly, flopping down onto the sofa next to her. 'He must be mad.'

'Yeah, yeah. Shall I press play?'

I nodded, pulling a blanket over my legs and trying not to feel too smug.

I really shouldn't have felt smug at all, my triumph was so short-lived. I replied to Freddie a cool two days later, and never heard from him again. Whew, what a rollercoaster.

'Maybe he's dead,' Beth told me brightly, swilling red wine around the bottom of her glass. We were sitting in one of those bars where you have to choose your wine from a dispenser and pay using a token. The whole process was stupidly unnecessarily and incredibly anxiety-inducing, in my books. One of those London things that just doesn't need to exist. 'Or he went to Spain and his phone got crushed by a bull,' she went on. 'Or, um …'

'It's okay,' I laughed. 'I'm not that cut up about it, really.'

Well, I couldn't be, could I? After all, I did understand his silence. There was no coming back from what I'd done to his poor penis.

I also didn't feel particularly wounded because of The Hair. That hair in his bed didn't indicate that he spent many nights with the same woman; I was just another girl he'd ghosted after a night of fun. And maybe that was okay, because it went both ways. I didn't see myself in a committed relationship with Freddie, and I'd got exactly what I needed from him at the time. A bit of lightness, a bit of humour, and a reminder of how idiotic and exhilarating dating could be. It might have been a bit ick, but it wasn't the end of the world.

'I just feel kind of embarrassed,' I told Beth. Pausing, I raised my glass to my lips. 'What's the most embarrassing thing you've done in bed?' I asked, desperate for some schadenfreude.

'Oh, boy.' She sat back in her seat, smiling wide at the ceiling. 'The most embarrassing thing I've done in bed? Um … probably giving a guy a sexy dance and then falling *off* the bed.'

I smirked. 'That's great, but not nearly as embarrassing as what I did.'

'I don't think anything could be, mate.'

A month after Freddie and I slept together, I completed my Caffè Nero loyalty card and chalked the whole thing up to experience. Another date, another anecdote. Then I returned to my desk, absent-mindedly clicked a link, and nearly sprayed my screen with the coffee I'd just bought. Suddenly, there Freddie was, haunting me in the form of a banner ad. 'Join me at 8 a.m.!' his static grin commanded.

'Already done that,' I muttered. And with a weak laugh, I closed the tab.

CHAPTER 8

Harry

With the departure of summer came a departure from dating, at least for a while. I needed a break. 'And what's a break for you?' Layla scoffed from the opposite desk. 'One week? Two?'

I frowned at her, but couldn't deny that I *had* become something of a serial dater these past few months. Even with all the bad experiences, there was something addictive about dating. It was like pulling the handle on a slot machine – time and again you got so close to what you were looking for: a fun, mutually fulfilling fling or a fragrant, blossoming romance. And every time you came up with two lemons and an orange (I'm not really sure how slot machines work), you thought: *Damn! But I'll get it next time. Just one more go ...*

So I can't pretend that I stopped dating altogether for two months – there were one or two forgettable drinks here and there. But for the most part I put the dating apps in a box, closed the lid and turned my key in the lock. For September and October, I generally stopped talking to strangers and put my sex life on hold. I really needed a break, I tipsily told increasingly weary friends.

So went autumn, and then November rolled around. Feeling revived, I decided to give dating another go. 'Just a couple more tries,' I muttered to myself. 'I can stop at any time.'

It's tricky to pin down what I wanted from dating at this point. As rollicking as my night with Freddie had been, again I had mixed feelings about being so disposable. Just another girl with blonde hair. Another day of the week.

I'd once wanted to be the female equivalent of Joey from *Friends* or Barney from *How I Met Your Mother*; someone who rolled in and out of other people's beds without a care. But after all I'd been through this year, that ambition was looking more and more unrealistic. Because even though Freddie hadn't attacked me or crossed any lines, I couldn't deny that he'd left me feeling a *little* empty, just as all the other men had.

'It sometimes feels like I'm on a conveyor belt,' I grumbled to Lizzie over the phone.

And so, again, I began to crave something different. Something more serious, more solid. Someone who wouldn't be a flash in the pan; a skittish, fickle, one-time fling. In other words, I had reverted to my pre-James attitude of wanting a boyfriend.

With very little hope left, I re-downloaded Hinge in the first week of November and stumbled across a month-old message from Harry. Immediately, I stopped in my tracks. Staring up at me was a handsome blonde with very blue eyes and delicate, elven features. Smouldering in a professional portrait, he said in his profile that he was an advertising creative. Okay, I thought, this is promising.

Hey! Sorry for my slow reply, I typed. *I deleted my Hinge for a bit. I'm good though, thanks. How's it going with you?*

Nerves crept in as I waited for his reply. I wondered if my own had been too slow and whether I'd missed the boat. Then my phone dinged from the top of the toilet. Drying one hand with a towel on the floor, I sat up in the bath and read his message. It was long, thoughtful and funny. I smiled, intrigued.

Do you want to go for a drink this week? he asked a few days later.

Sure, I said, aiming for nonchalance though my heart was skipping. *Do you live near Kentish Town?*

Harry was clearly nervous when we met at Camden Town station. Wrinkling and unwrinkling his face as we walked, he buried his hands in his pockets and spoke with too much sincerity. Zipping up my leather jacket, I concealed a grin. It was sweet. He was only an inch taller than me in heels and had such piercing, flitting eyes. He reminded me of a little bird.

Eventually we found a small space in the garden at the Hawley Arms, fairy lights swaying overhead.

'Are you warm enough?' Harry asked when we sat down. 'Would you like my coat?'

'No,' I laughed. 'I'm already wearing one. And what would you wear? You'd be freezing.'

'Oh, please don't insult me,' Harry joked, holding up his hands. 'I'm clearly a very masculine, hot-blooded man.'

The more we drank and laughed, the more his nerves melted away. He told me about the perils of working in advertising, shaking a fist at 'the man who came up with those bastard meerkats'. I told him about the possible porn director at work, and shared examples of peculiar ex-flatmates, of which I had several.

'So this one guy at uni would roast a whole chicken every day,' I told him. 'With nothing else. No garnish, no gravy, nothing. He'd just sling a chicken into the oven and then carry the tray to his room.'

'*No.*' Harry threw his head back as he laughed, nearly knocking it on the brick wall behind us. 'He'd take the tray and eat a whole, plain chicken in his room?'

'That's right. Every day, without fail.' I paused, sucking my straw. 'But he was nothing compared to another flatmate I had, who ate pizza with ketchup every dinner and dipped his biscuits into orange juice.'

'*Orange juice?*' Harry paled.

'Yeah. Even chocolate digestives, sometimes.'

'Fuck me. That's grim.'

We grinned at each other, pleasantly surprised by how much fun we were having. After three rum and cokes, our conversation turned conspiratorial.

'You see that couple over there?' Harry muttered, nodding towards the other end of the garden. 'They're definitely on a first date.'

'Yeah, you're probably right.' I winced. 'It does look pretty awkward.'

'Yup. They haven't spoken in about five minutes.'

'Yeesh.'

'But look at us! We're doing so much better than they are,' Harry beamed. Emboldened, he slung an arm around my shoulders. 'Honestly, as first dates go,' he told me, 'I think we're doing pretty well.'

I looked up at his sweet, handsome face, mushy inside. He was right. This date couldn't be going any better. Everything felt so easy with him. So natural. I felt like I'd known him for years, which was a bizarre, exhilarating, and completely new feeling.

'You're so beautiful,' Harry said in a low voice, looking at me steadily. I was surprised: this was the first really, really flirty thing he'd said all night. I bit my tongue slightly, my heart quickening. After a pause, he added: 'Would it be okay if I kissed you?'

I laughed. 'Sure.'

And oof – it was an exceptional first kiss: soft but passionate, Harry's hand trailing up the back of my neck. His other one found my thigh and gripped onto it.

When he pulled away, Harry looked at me carefully.

'Have we met before?'

'I don't think so,' I replied, my heart jumping.

Tucking a curl behind my ear, he eyed me with suspicion.

'Not a work thing? Or a mutual friend's thing?'

I shook my head.

'Weird. It definitely feels like I've met you before.'

'I know,' I agreed nervously, heat creeping up into my face. 'I feel that way, too.'

Once Harry and I started kissing, it was quite hard to stop. I could see the wary eyes of waiters and the lingering gaze of an old man sitting alone with his pint, but I didn't care. Wrapped up in this strangely familiar man's jacket, his tongue in my mouth, I decided that I wanted him. Tonight.

By 11 p.m. there seemed to be an unspoken consensus between us. Harry asked me if I lived nearby, and we picked up our bags and left.

I smirked in the corner shop where he awkwardly bought condoms, shying away from the white, overhead lights. That specific transaction is always entertaining to watch. The man at the till had been cool and uninterested when Harry approached, his palms flat on the counter, shoulders sloped. But when Harry hesitantly mentioned Durex, it was like a bolt ran through him. Suddenly the man was standing very straight and not looking Harry in the eye.

'There you go, mate.'

'Great. Thanks, mate.'

'Mate' being the life raft for men in such situations. I told Harry this as we boarded the tube and he nodded, laughing.

'It's true, you know,' he admitted. 'We all have a quota of "mate"s to bring out in condom conversations. I think I've maxed mine out tonight.'

He kept his arm around my shoulders on the tube, and I looked at another couple at the end of the carriage. The man's arm was also around the woman's shoulder, breaking the path of white-blonde rivulets trickling down her back. How long have they been together? I wondered. And how long do they think *we've* been together? Glancing up at Harry, who was deconstructing the ad above our heads, I smiled. They'd never imagine just one date, I decided. We really were doing well.

Chuckling at something inane, I shushed Harry as I let him into my flat. He crept after me into the bedroom, then sat down on the bed with a strange air of formality.

'You alright?' I laughed, sitting down beside him.

'Yeah.' Harry turned to face me, pulling his legs onto the bed. 'It's just … I don't know. I just can't believe we're doing this, I suppose.' He laughed awkwardly.

'Now, you mean? On the first date?'

'Yeah.' His smile fading, Harry nodded solemnly. I blinked at the carpet, feeling slightly ashamed.

'Oh, well, we don't have to if you don't want to.'

'No, no!' Harry took my wrists, shaking his head. 'Honestly, I don't mean … don't take it like that, Kitty. I really, *really* want to. And … you do too, right?'

'Yeah.' I nodded, half-chuckling.

'Well, then.' Harry paused, looking at me in the same mesmerising, careful way he'd looked at me at the pub. 'Then I think we should, you know. It's kind of amazing really …'

He didn't finish the thought, leaning forward to kiss me instead. Gently pushing me down onto the mattress, Harry straddled my waist, cupping my face in his hands while he kissed my mouth, then my jaw, then my neck. Heat prickled up through my body, coiling and uncoiling in my chest.

We had sex three times that night. It was unbelievably good. His body seemed to have been moulded for mine, which came as a surprise when I saw his penis. No way is that getting inside me, I thought.

He smirked when he saw my reaction. 'It's bigger than people expect,' he said with barely contained pride.

I nodded, looking up at him. 'No offence, but you don't give off big dick energy.'

Harry laughed, taking none, and four orgasms later I lay on his chest, tracing a finger up and down his arm. I liked how we were lying here, slotted together like the last two pieces of a puzzle. Looking up into his happy eyes, I tried very hard not to say this out loud. We were silent for a few moments, and then:

'That's Hollywood, baby!' he proclaimed out of the blue.

And I laughed, thinking that I'd found my soulmate.

———————◆———————

All of that comfort and familiarity grew and blossomed over the next few months. On our third date we had period sex, something I'd never done before.

I started a few minutes before going out to meet him – cursing my uterus and the red stain in my lacy underwear.

Sex was off the cards, I thought with remorse. Boys don't like blood.

As it happened, however, Harry wasn't fazed.

'I don't mind if you don't,' he shrugged, my hand on his chest, one leg bent around his. 'It's up to you, but I'm down.'

Minutes later, I looked up at his bloodstained torso with newfound respect. The sex was amazing, too. Even better than last time.

Everything, in fact, became better with time. Each date blew the last one out the water. We laughed more, we talked more, we learnt more about each other. I tousled his hair and he remembered how I liked my coffee in the morning. Evenings and sleepovers became sprawling weekends, my phone buzzing with messages from friends asking where I'd been and what I'd been doing. Drinks at a pub became tea over breakfast, then a walk around Hyde Park and more drinks and more dinner.

On a midweek morning we'd share a shower, leaving for work together. Then we'd split off at the bottom of the road, kissing each other with the brusqueness of a married couple. And every time we parted ways, I'd walk away with the same immovable smile. I'd bathe in the afterglow of our weekend together, warmed to the core.

In short, I was finally falling in love. If I'd felt something burgeoning with James, I felt something even stronger for Harry. One night we crossed paths with his flatmate, also on a date, and the four of us sat chatting in Harry's living room for a few minutes – two smug couples smiling at each other in the candlelight.

And just like that, I became part of a two. My desire for hot-blooded, wild sex with strangers fell away. All of a sudden, I wanted to be in a committed relationship with Harry. I was a changed woman! I wanted him to be in my future, and fantasised that, one day, he'd tell me that he was also falling in love, his anxious blue eyes watching mine. The idea that he might actually do this made my heart flutter.

I felt a closeness with him I'd never felt with anyone else, and so – three months in – I decided to tell him my deepest, most closely guarded secret.

We were walking to Portobello Road, somewhere along the more desolate streets of Westbourne Park.

Taking my hand, Harry smiled down at me. 'So, personal question,' he began, swinging our hands between us as we walked. 'When did you lose your virginity?'

Looking at the pavement, my mind went blank. Pausing, I bit my lip, and wondered whether I should lie. I'd lied to almost all of my friends about this, shame-facedly saying that I'd had sex at eighteen at a party. I'd told the same lie to every man who had ever asked, too.

But I didn't want to lie to Harry, I discovered. For the first time, I didn't feel the need to.

'Twenty-two,' I eventually replied, cutting my eyes at him.

He stared back at me and stopped in the street, blinking twice in surprise.

'Twenty-two?' he repeated. With a brief nod, he resumed walking. 'Wow! That's ... er, so late.'

'Yeah, alright,' I chuckled, giving him a little shove. 'How old were you?'

'Fifteen.' He was chuckling now as well. 'But wait.' Harry tugged my hand and willed me to look at him. 'How come you waited so long? That means you've only been having sex for what, two, three years?'

With a deep breath, I decided to continue down this path of honesty, which was beginning to feel a little unsteady.

'Well, yeah.'

'How come?'

'I was a bit, er … scarred,' I told him softly, eyeing the pavement again. 'And yeah, sorry, this is probably way too much, but …' My heart was pounding. 'Well, I felt a bit messed up about sex because I was sexually assaulted when I was ten.'

I watched Harry pale slightly, a quiet suddenly descending between us. I wasn't sure if the silence was good or bad, or if telling him had been the right thing to do. Shit. Had it been the right thing to do?

'So it was a ten-year-old who did it,' I went on. 'He said he was my boyfriend, and that this was what girlfriends did for their boyfriends, and I said no, but …'

Harry looked at me, his expression oddly unreadable.

'Well, I figured I didn't really have a choice,' I shrugged.

'Fuck.' He squeezed my hand.

'Sorry.' I found myself laughing suddenly, shaking my head. 'It's probably a bit much. But yeah, I only really started acknowledging it a few months ago. Before that, I always thought I was a virgin at 22 because I was frigid and weird. But I wasn't, well … anyway, sorry.'

Harry also started shaking his head, but his shaking was more vehement. 'No, stop apologising. Look, I'm so, *so* sorry that happened to you. And thank you for sharing. But don't apologise, please. You don't need to.'

He turned me round to face him again, leafless branches waving at me from behind his head.

'Okay?' Harry prompted, his eyes soft and steady.

I nodded, tears suddenly pooling in mine. Then he pulled me in for a warm, tight hug. When he released me, Harry gave me a deep, tender kiss, the deepest he'd ever given me. *You're not broken*, it told me. *And you're not spoiled goods. This won't change anything and it isn't too much.*

He held me close that night, and I buried my face into the crook of his arm, so glad I'd told him.

———————◆———————

Still, what I told him wasn't even the half of it. I didn't tell Harry about ripping up my old diaries in case they contained a trace of the event, assuring myself it had been a dream. I didn't tell him about the fear which seemed to lurk everywhere I looked: how I hid by the front door or under the kitchen table when my 'boyfriend' called round.

I didn't tell him about crying on a taster day at my secondary school because, unexpectedly, he was there, too. 'What's the matter?' a kind-faced teacher had asked me, her hand on my shoulder. I said I didn't know, and I really, really didn't.

I also didn't tell Harry that the experience had given me a hand tremor and vulvodynia, a condition which only antidepressants would fix. That every day for years, my knees would buckle – my crotch in searing pain. That sometimes I'd wake up to electric currents coursing down my vulva, and would wince when I had to wash it in the shower, or when the bus went over a speed bump. Praying that nobody noticed, I'd cross my legs tightly and grit my teeth.

I didn't tell him about the countless hours spent seeing doctors and dermatologists, who couldn't tell me what was wrong.

Nor did I tell him that I'd been morbidly afraid of men for a long, long time, or about the damage of pinning all of my fears on being 'frigid and weird', which bred its own set of social anxieties. That, and the feeling that I wasn't good enough. That I was an oddball and an outcast and a fuck-up.

But I told him everything I needed him to know in that moment, and it was a lot more than I'd told most people. In that moment I felt so grateful for Harry. So thankful that I'd met him, such a kind, empathetic, sensitive person.

———————

That being said, there were some low points in the relationship, too. There was one thing that really bothered me, and that was how often he mentioned his ex-girlfriend. She drifted into conversation as early as the second date.

'Kitty, do you know why I wanted to go back to your place last time?' he asked me, naked in bed.

'No?' I replied, looking up at him curiously. *Did he need a reason?*

'Well, it was because I was living with my ex at the time.'

'Oh.' The word sounded small in my mouth. Looking away in thought, I took a moment to absorb this information. Eventually, I asked: 'So, then ... when did you guys break up?'

'At the end of October.'

'At the end of October? Oh ... okay.'

Well, shit. When I did the maths, I realised that he'd gone on his first date with me a week later. *One week later.* My heart sank, and I looked back at him warily. *Surely you're not ready for a relationship,* I wanted to say. *Go on, just tell me that I'm a rebound.* But I saw the expression in his eyes, nervous and affectionate, and a quiet voice said: *Maybe he is ready. Maybe I'm not a rebound …*

The more I grew to like him – love him, even – the tighter I clung onto this hope. But as the weeks went by, she cropped up more and more often. He spoke about her with increasing vitriol, his delicate face hardening in a way which made it look wrong and unfamiliar, his tone uncharacteristically acidic.

She'd left the flat in a state, he complained. She'd made him take up smoking because she stressed him out so much. Worst of all, she'd cheated on him with her boss at work.

'Shit,' I breathed. 'That's awful.'

'Yep,' he nodded, tying his laces at the foot of the bed.

'Well, what did you do? What did you say?'

I couldn't see his face, but heard him quietly chuckle.

'I spat in her face,' Harry said proudly.

From his voice, it sounded like he was smiling, and I felt myself recoil. He'd *spat in her face*? I repeated to myself. Alarm bells suddenly started to sound, telling me that of *course* this had been too good to be true. Of course he was as messed up as the rest of them.

It wasn't good, what he'd just said. It wasn't good at all. Sure, he'd been angry, but there was something degrading about spitting in someone's face. Humiliating. What if he did that to me one day?

'Well, exactly,' Elle agreed at work the next week. 'And, more importantly, I just don't get why he'd tell *you* that.'

I nodded. I didn't know either. But as time wore on I shrugged it off, deciding that you didn't really know what went on in someone else's relationship. Maybe I couldn't judge what he'd said or done in the heat of the moment. After all, how could I know what was normal in a relationship, having never been in one?

Crucially, I also wanted to believe that I was different. He'd split up with her a broken man, and I'd arrived just in time to scoop him up, put him back together, and restore his faith in women. Gradually, misogyny bled from his words into my brain. She was a crazy, psycho bitch, but I wasn't.

Over time, I conspired with Harry, sharing in his anger. It wasn't entirely for his sake. To my shame, his portrayal of her made me feel better about myself. Things had been turbulent with her, but Harry felt safe and calm and self-assured with me. She made him feel terrible about himself; I made him happy. So maybe what we had was real, I told myself. Maybe he was into it as much as I was. Maybe we'd be together for months, years and ... who knows, maybe even for life?

I ignored the many signs to the contrary, the most glaring being that I never knew where I stood with Harry. Not really. One moment he'd be so romantic, so dedicated, and the next he'd go off the radar. On one occasion, he told me that he wanted to record me playing guitar so that he could listen to it when he missed me, plugging a cable into the base and watching me awkwardly pluck a C chord. His expression had been so fond, but when I let him know that I was home safe the next morning, he didn't reply for three days.

In December, Harry disappeared for a month-long road trip up north, promising to send me a postcard from each city. I swooned, but the postcards never came. I hardly heard a thing from him during this time, and felt so disappointed I began dating other people.

'Nothing from Tour of the North?' Elle asked me one morning, handing Layla and I cups of tea. 'Tour of the North' was her new name for Harry. An actual northerner, she found it endlessly amusing that someone would spend a month traipsing around its cities.

'Nothing,' I told her, feigning a smile. 'I haven't heard a peep.'

She frowned but, an eternal optimist, shrugged. 'Oh, well. He might be busy. We won't cross him off yet!'

Sadly, her optimism about Harry didn't endure. His promises turned out to be hot air because, in truth, his feelings for me didn't go that deep. How could they when he still felt so much for someone else?

Maybe I was never his girlfriend. Maybe I was the cork he was using to bottle up his feelings. A distraction from the trauma of a very painful break-up. As clear as that is now, I refused to see it at the time. I liked him too much.

No period of silence from Harry was more gut-wrenching than the last one, the one that finished us off. Reconnecting after Christmas (and his tour of the north), he and I began to date again, and it was in January that I told him about being assaulted as a child. A week later, Harry went quiet. Days and days elapsed, and nothing. It was devastating.

Eventually, I found myself initiating a conversation, though doing so made me feel desperate and embarrassed. He responded in his usual funny tone, but was cagey. I could read between the lines. And when the back-and-forth began to die, he let it. Checking my phone for a message from him became an act of self-flagellation. I wanted one so badly – it could have been about the weather or the traffic or the sandwich he'd eaten for lunch – but nothing came. I winced at the blank screen, time and time again. When I woke up, when I sat down on the bus, when I came back from a meeting at work.

'Well, why don't *you* message *him*?' Lizzie asked reasonably, putting me on speakerphone while she diced a pepper.

Silently, I shook my head, staring out of my bedroom window at some wobbling leaves outside.

'If he wanted to talk to me, he'd talk to me,' I said glumly.

And finally, as January came to a close, he did. After two weeks of radio silence, Harry booty-called me.

Hey Kitty, what are you up to tonight? he asked, 6pm on a Saturday. *Do you want to come round mine?*

I looked down at my phone and laughed a short, mirthless laugh. The word 'Rebound' lit up in front of me in blue, neon letters, and this time I couldn't look away. We both wanted such different things from each other – that was what was so painful. Clearly he was fond of me; clearly he liked me, but I was a fun weekend to him, while this was the beginning of a relationship to me. I was a girl he liked to have sex with; he was the man I was falling in love with.

And I couldn't believe it. I couldn't believe that I'd been so stupid not to see that. So idiotic to develop feelings for someone so obviously detached; to spill my guts to him; to fantasise about a future with him. Oh God, why had I ignored all the signs?

Running a hand over my face, I sighed at the ceiling. When friends would coo and ask for updates about Harry, I'd have to tell them that I'd got it all wrong. Shaking my head, I felt a hot wave of humiliation. God, how had I been so *stupid*? Why had I told so many people about him?

Oh well, it was done now. I'd have to face them eventually, and I'd have to think of what to reply to Harry …

'Don't reply at all!' Maisie told me over a pint. My other friends echoed this sentiment, and I had to admit that it was probably wise. The man had ghosted me for two weeks, swinging back into my life to ask for sex. It was disrespectful, right? He didn't deserve a response, did he? I knew this was a sensible line of thought, but, oh, cutting ties was hard. Quiet tears slid into my pillowcase that night as I tried to fall asleep, his booty call unanswered. I suppressed a gentle flow of happy memories, misguided hope blooming in my chest. I knew that I'd have to pull that hope from the ground, painful as it was. All for the miserable reason that I deserved better.

Months later, when I started writing this book, I heard from him again.

Hey Kitty, how are you? Harry asked in May 2020, adding cryptically: *I actually decided to move up north in February. *Sweat drop emoji*.*

Again, I let out a hollow laugh. I supposed this was his way of explaining the two-week silence. Maybe he'd had a lot going on, but he could have dropped me a ten-word message to let me know, surely?

So once again, I didn't reply. I was tempted to, but held fire. The damage was done, I decided. It was just a few months too late.

Do I regret not replying, now? A little. Not to his booty-call message (I still don't think that deserved a response), but as for the second message … With retrospect I wish I'd told him how much his silence had hurt me; how I'd opened up to him and developed feelings for him and he'd responded by ignoring then booty-calling me. I also regret not wishing him well, and saying that I hoped things in his life were good. I don't feel any anger towards him now, nor resentment. I only feel that he was a little sad and fragmented when we were dating, though he did a good job – for the most part – of hiding it.

Maybe he was trying to put his life back together and found that it looked jarringly different to how it had looked before. Maybe he wasn't ready to build another story only for it to be torn up again. Maybe he did feel something for me, but was confused and anxious and scared.

But that's the thing about dating apps. They throw you together with people who are looking for something, ready or not. And if you arrive at the destination before they do, you might find yourself waiting on the platform alone.

I wish, in a way, that I hadn't done to him exactly what he did to me. I might have felt a sense of triumph at the time, but I don't feel that now. He should have taught me that ghosting is one of the worst things you can do to someone, unless there's a good reason why that person doesn't deserve a response.

Because being ghosted is an awful, awful experience. I know that now, truly. Harry exposed me to the nauseating, quivering hope that I'd wake up to a reply, only to find renewed humiliation in the morning, the dinging of my phone with a message from everyone other than him. The lingering fear that dogged me whenever I started dating someone new, telling me not to get too invested because it might happen again. The fear that I might get left alone again, just as I was on the cusp of being in love.

Many of my friends have been ghosted. But what made me feel even more alone, at the time, was that no one admitted to it.

'Are you still seeing x?' I'd ask.

'No,' they'd reply, averting their eyes.

'Oh, why not?'

'Eh, it just fizzled out. I can't actually remember who sent the last message.'

But they *could*. Of course they could. I could tell in the way they'd look down, suddenly self-conscious. Writing this chapter, I typed 'ghosted' into YouTube and found videos with millions of views, their subjects talking about being ghosted after four dates, four months, four *years*.

'Lizzie,' I said, pressing my phone to my ear, one hand hovering over my keyboard. 'I've just watched a video where a girl talks about being ghosted by her *husband*.'

'Her husband?'

'Yeah. He just disappeared from her life for a year for no reason.'

'God.' There was particular emphasis on the 'd'.

'Crazy, right?' I shook my head. 'No one is safe!'

'No,' she agreed solemnly. 'Except ... do you think ghosting is ever okay? I feel kind of bad, but I've done it before.'

I paused, thinking about it. Was there ever a 'genuinely good excuse' to ghost someone? 'Well, yeah, if someone's done something awful or disrespectful,' I conceded. 'Or if someone's not taking "no" for an answer, I guess. Like that guy who kept messaging you about galleon cakes.'

Lizzie snorted. I could hear her put her hand to her forehead. 'Yeah, I mean ... what would I even have said to that?'

'Nothing.' I lifted my eyebrows. 'So I suppose sometimes it's okay.'

A few nights later, I canvassed other friends for their opinions.

'Ghosting before the third date is fine,' Lydia said authoritatively, blowing smoke out of the corner of her mouth. 'After that, you have to break up over coffee.'

'Coffee?' another friend howled, staring from the depths of her puffa jacket. 'Oh, no, there's nothing worse than that. If someone took me for a break-up coffee three dates into the relationship, I'd tell them to fuck off.'

As the conversation moved on and we went inside, I considered my mojito, none the wiser. Was ghosting sometimes the kinder thing to do? You wouldn't put the other person through the humiliation of being dumped in public; you wouldn't force them to choke back tears on the way home – you'd allow the dumpee's tears to flow freely in the privacy of their own bedroom. The same could be achieved with a text message, but at least ghosting meant that they could tell their friends that you were a cowardly prick who didn't deserve them.

But no. Deep down, I knew that there was nothing more humiliating than being ignored; than apparently being unworthy of an explanation. Thinking about it at length, I felt a sharp regret for my own ghostings.

It's weird – in a time when we have more ways than ever to talk to each other, so many of us choose silence instead. I suppose it's the easier option, for one person at least. But it's not the kindest option by any means. In the comments under one of the YouTube videos I was watching, one stood out in particular: 'What a sad, lonely generation.'

That sums it up.

So, all in all, I'm grateful to Harry for teaching me to never ghost again, not without serious consideration, at least. I'm also just grateful for him in general. Though the end was bitter, we had some sunny times and some top-notch sex. He was also the longest relationship I'd ever had, and the beginning of the discovery that I *could* have relationships, in addition to sex; that there were kind men out there, though they were flawed, and that I could really one day fall in love.

CHAPTER 9

Ollie

Well, that wouldn't happen for a while yet. First there'd be Ollie, who I started dating in December. It was during Harry's first stint of silence, when he ventured off on his tour of the north. He and I had been on eight dates at this point (the rest taking place in January), but I suspected I might not hear from him again. To patch myself up, I decided to go on a date with a man called Ollie.

I considered myself pretty jaded at this point; completely cynical about a woman's ability to have exhilarating, care-free sex with strangers. There would be no turning the horse around this late into the game, I thought gloomily; no last-minute attempts to become Samantha, or any other fictional character for that matter. I was no longer convincing myself that such a thing was possible. On top of that, I had zero confidence in my ability to build a more meaningful relationship with someone.

Still, so much sex had done something strange to me. I needed it now, just as I needed my cup of coffee in the morning or a glass of wine at the end of the week. It was a delicious hit; a quick way to feel something. The only thing that sent currents through my body and cleared my mind for a few lucid, blissful moments. That's all dating and sex was to me now: a euphoric rush and a break from my own internal dialogue.

And to get over the disappointment of Harry, I had to get under someone else.

I met Ollie on Hinge, of course. He was handsome and tall and eccentric; a jaded, funny, out-of-work actor and occasional comedian with dark shadows under his eyes. He was also ten years my senior, which only added to my intrigue. I'd never dated someone in their *mid*-thirties.

In person, my attraction to him was instantaneous. One moment I was pushing against the door of a heaving little pub, the next I was sucked into a laughing, chattering crowd, and I saw him. His face had a magnetic force, pulling me through the throng to meet him at the bar.

'Hello,' he said, pulling me in for a hug.

'Hullo,' I replied, smiling back at him. It was odd. I felt strangely at ease.

What made me even more attracted to Ollie was that he was a bit of a dick. I discovered this after we carried our G & Ts to the conservatory – the same conservatory I'd sat in a year ago, with my first one-night stand. How much had changed during that time, I thought, looking around. And yet the room had stayed exactly the same.

Ollie took the measure of me when we sat down and, at the earliest opportunity, started digging me out. I said something self-deprecating about work and he ran with the narrative, laughing at my 'stopgap job'. Later, when I missed the straw with my mouth, he stared at me.

'You alright there?' he asked, his face splitting into a grin.

'Yes.' I felt my own redden as I took hold of the straw and drank. Ollie said nothing, continuing to watch me with the same smile plastered across his face. 'Shut up,' I added out of the corner of my mouth.

He chuckled. 'Are you nervous?'

'No.' Oh God, that sounded very defensive. Nonchalantly, I added: 'Why … are you nervous?'

Ollie shook his head.

'No. Not at all.'

Hm, I believed him. This man was brazen.

Maybe, deep down, I was looking for the antithesis to Harry, who had always been so gentle and attentive. Ollie certainly wasn't the type to ask if he could kiss you; he started touching me twenty minutes into our date, his hand on my knee as I spoke about my week. Minutes later it moved up to my thigh, which he rubbed when he laughed.

I could see in his face that he enjoyed how this act distracted me. How it sucked the next sentence out of my mouth, my mind suddenly blank.

'What's up?' he taunted on one occasion, inching towards my hemline.

Ollie was even more tactile when he was rude. At one point we were talking about going to the gym and I told him I'd only been once. I gestured to my noodle arms disparagingly, and he nodded in agreement.

'Yeah, I can tell,' he said.

'Right. Thanks.'

Ollie snickered, grabbing both noodles and pulling me towards him. All of a sudden my legs were wedged between his. I looked down at them, my face hot. It was bold and brash, but it was also intoxicating, this feeling of being wanted by a stranger in the middle of a busy pub. He didn't care about the fact that we'd just met or that people might roll their eyes. It was the boost my ego needed, having spent days wondering whether Harry had had enough of me.

Ollie and I were ousted from the table an hour later.

'Reserved?' he repeated with mock outrage, standing as if he was about to lay down a gauntlet. 'Well, fine then,' he told the man standing awkwardly with his party. 'We'll go elsewhere. Happy birthday ...' Ollie looked down at the card on the table. '*Bill*.'

The poor man offered him a bemused smile, and Ollie led me away. I felt similarly bemused, but too tipsy to cringe.

Our only other option was a loveseat wedged beside an enormous Christmas tree.

'That'll do,' he said, pulling me down beside him.

I looked up at the angel, crooked where she met the ceiling, and smiled. Ollie disappeared to the bar for another round, and I watched the white lights shine steadfastly, carols warbling through the speakers in the corner.

I'd taken a single sip of my drink when Ollie kissed me. Hm. His kiss was fervent and wet, just a little too enthusiastic. It was off-putting at first, but the more I guided him with my tongue, the more he eased into the kiss. It became less awkward, more effortless, my right hand tightening around his thick, dark hair.

Okay, yeah – this was getting good. Very good.

'You know,' Ollie said, peeling away. 'I don't think I'll be able to leave you tonight, Kitty. I think ...'

He paused, lowering his voice and boring his brown eyes into me. 'I think tonight will have to be a *naughty night*.'

I laughed awkwardly in response, wanting to die. I should pick up my coat and leave right now, I thought, everything inside me twisting with embarrassment. But his eyes had a look of longing that was hard to reject ...

'Er, maybe,' I mumbled, my own on the floor. 'I don't know.'

'Well, I wasn't saying we have to do *that*,' Ollie said quietly, pulling me closer. I glanced up at his face, faintly impressed by how undeterred he was. 'We could just get dinner somewhere if you want. I know a great little Italian place around the corner.'

'Oh yeah? Well, okay ... that sounds good.'

'Great!'

Standing, Ollie helped me into my coat.

But when we stepped outside, my inhibitions deserted me. He kissed me again, his hands in my hair, and I suddenly realised how cold it was. Blistering. The idea of cuddling up to a warm body in a heated apartment was suddenly too tantalising.

Smiling, Ollie read my mind.

'Shall I get us an Uber?' he muttered, pulling me into his long coat.

And I nodded, my arms around his waist.

***

I was quiet in the Uber, watching street lamps and hunched figures flurry by. Ollie discussed football with the driver – a conversation I couldn't partake in – but felt for my hand when we arrived. I took it, smiling down at my boots.

Rounding the car, Ollie led me towards a row of identical buildings. Polished and modern, each apartment fronted onto a balcony with clear walls and thoughtfully arranged plants.

I stared up at them as we walked, thinking that they looked a bit like show homes.

Stepping into the lift after him, I glanced at Ollie doubtfully. How could an out-of-work actor afford this? I wondered. Did he have an inheritance? Was he secretly rich? Had he been in a blockbuster I'd never seen, years ago?

I became even more suspicious when we walked into his apartment. It was enormous: three times the size of my own. Running a finger along the glass coffee table, I wondered what was most impressive: the flat-screen TV, the floor-to-ceiling windows, or the black piano tucked into a corner.

'Nice place,' I announced as he handed me a glass of wine. I cleared my throat and attempted my best Larry David impression. 'Pr-etty, pr-etty good.'

Ollie smirked, rolling his eyes.

'Yeah, I guess,' he shrugged. 'I'm looking to move out soon.'

Then he pulled me into his lap.

'Woah.' I laughed, steadying my glass. 'This'll leave a stain, you know.'

Smiling, Ollie took it from my hand and placed it on the table, lifting my jumper up over my head.

'Nice dress,' he muttered, watching his hands move across the velvet. 'Pr-etty, pr-etty good.' Then he leaned down to kiss me, cutting my laughter short.

We stayed like that for a few moments before he manoeuvred me round to straddle him. I looked down at his eyes, suddenly very aware of his erection, and he pushed my face down to meet his, his tongue in my mouth. After a couple of minutes he breathed a soft, happy sigh. 'This is so relaxing,' he said, our lips parting. 'Just what I needed after a long week. But ... do you know what would make me even more relaxed?'

I paused, resting back on my haunches. 'No?' I said, my hands on his stomach.

'A bath.' Ollie nodded, smiling to himself. 'Yeah. Hold on, I'll go and run one.'

And with that he rolled me back onto the sofa. I sat up, watching him leave the room, and a moment later heard the squeak of a tap.

My phone lit up with a message from Jen at the same time. I grabbed it.

'How's it going?' she asked.

'Good,' I typed with furious speed. 'I'm back at his.'

'OOOH. Have fun!'

'It's a bit weird, though.' My thumbs were a blur. 'He's just gone to run a bath.'

'A bath?'

Suddenly, Ollie appeared at the door. I put my phone away sheepishly.

'Come on,' he grinned, beckoning me over.

Unsure of what to do or say, I followed him to the bathroom in silence. Oh God, I thought, crossing the threshold. It seemed like he'd been planning on doing this all along. Steam rose from the water, tealight flames swaying, and Brigitte Bardot trilled and cooed from the speakers by the sink. As Ollie pulled the velvet dress over my head, I wondered if she'd ever shared a bath with someone she'd known for three hours. Probably not.

◆

Ollie undressed me first, then himself, and stepped gingerly into the tub. He pulled me in after him, my body on top of his.

Bubbles wafted from his hand as he pushed my hair aside, lowering his mouth to kiss my neck. And slowly, my reservations began to melt – this was quite nice, actually. Maybe it was fine. Maybe it wasn't too weird that I was sharing a bath with someone I'd literally just met. As his hands snaked down to my waist, I closed my eyes.

Okay. This was very, very nice.

Keen to return the favour, I twisted round to face him. Slowly and deliberately, I left a trail of kisses down Ollie's wet chest, stomach and navel until I came face-to-face with his penis, which was very erect and pretty impressive. But when I began the favour in earnest, there was a problem. The more excited Ollie became, the less control he had over his waist. It kept dropping into the water.

Not to be deterred, I dove in after it. Surely underwater blow jobs are a thing, I thought. But alas, they're not, unless you have a snorkel. A few moments into fellatio I suddenly remembered that I needed to breathe, and emerged with a rush of bubbles.

'You okay?' he asked, half-amused.

'Yes,' I nodded, looking up at Ollie with bleary eyes. I wiped my mascara off with a flick.

He pulled the plug a few minutes later, wrapping me in a towel and slapping my arse.

'To the bedroom,' Ollie cried, blowing out candles as he went.

I padded after him down the hall, steam spilling out of the bathroom behind us. Were we actually going to have sex now? I thought hesitantly. I knew that was probably a stupid question to ask after we'd just been lying on top of each other, naked, but this felt like a further step. A step I wasn't sure I was ready to take.

Because, yes, we had chemistry. And yes, he was attractive. And I know: we'd just shared bathwater. But I'd also only known him for a handful of hours, and he was about to be *inside* me, which was a little different. I'd had sex on the first date many times before, but something about Ollie made me feel slightly … uncertain.

Blinking in the light of his bedroom, I decided that it was probably too late to change my mind. Well, I was here now. And I was naked.

'Alright, here we are,' Ollie announced, closing the door behind me. Holding the top of my towel, I took a cursory look around.

It felt like a room I'd stepped into many times before. Just like so many boys' bedrooms before it, Ollie's was plain and grey, the only splash of colour existing in the form of a laundry pile in the corner. The bed wasn't made properly, its limp duvet halfway on the floor, and there were only two pillows, which were crumpled and probably from IKEA.

'It's nice!' I said, smiling at them.

Ollie didn't reply. He just turned me round and opened my towel, looking me over and drying my body. Squeezing my wet hair in a fist, he pushed me down onto the mattress, opening my legs. And with his mouth on my thighs, I felt a little more certain about having sex with Ollie. Okay, I thought: I can do this. It doesn't matter that this is a slightly mad stranger who just put me in a bath. This is great. Yes, this is *great*.

It stayed great for a few minutes. I clung to the pillows as he gave me head, floppy and breathless in its aftermath. Then he planted a kiss in the crook of my neck and I shuddered, entwining his legs with mine. Yes, this is excellent, I thought. Exactly the release I'd needed. But I felt a renewed sense of hesitation when Ollie became bossy: telling me what to do and where to move. 'Move your legs there,' he'd say. Or: 'Turn and face the wall. Now come closer.' He was clearly getting a kick out of my compliance.

'I like how obedient you are,' he murmured into my ear at one point. 'I can make you do anything, can't I?'

That was a bit creepy, I thought with a grimace. And then, all of a sudden, he draped me across his lap and started spanking me, hard. Good God! I blinked. *Very* hard.

'Ah!' I winced, but this only encouraged him. Ollie kept going and going until an angry red handprint had formed.

Laughing at his handiwork, he proceeded to press me face-down on the bed. Then he began to finger me, and for a while, this was okay. Not nearly as good as the stuff before the spanking, but okay. Bearable. Until I felt his other hand wind around my neck.

Which was fine for a while, too, until I really, really couldn't breathe. My eyes on the pillow below me, I registered that I hadn't been able to breathe for almost ten seconds now. Ten seconds. *Fuck.* What was happening? Was I being murdered right now? Was I going to die?

Strangely, the thought didn't make me feel as panicked as it should have. Even more bizarrely, it made me feel calm. And just when I started to feel lightheaded, he let go. Ollie shifted me onto my side, wrapping his limbs around mine.

'Sorry,' he whispered into my neck, hugging me tightly. 'I think I might have gone a bit far there.'

'It's fine,' I lied, blinking in the dark.

———————

In the morning, Ollie pushed my head towards his penis. I got it over with, then yanked my clothes on and left for work.

He walked me to a bus stop a couple roads away, then leaned down to kiss me goodbye. It was a nice kiss, actually. He'd really improved in the space of a night.

From the top deck of the bus, I watched his retreating body and pulled out my phone. In a few stops' time I'd be in Kentish Town, walking to work in the same dress I'd worn last night.

'I'm going to work with cum in my hair, Jen,' I typed as the bus began to move. 'CUM IN MY HAIR.'

'Lol,' she replied.

'I can't believe I'm going to a work Christmas lunch with semen in my hair. Omg.'

'Well, was it fun at least? Give me the lowdown.'

I hesitated for a moment, then decided to tell her about the night with no holds barred. I told her about the bath and the spanking and the choking, but was surprised when she expressed sympathy.

'He sounds like a bad man,' Jen said. 'Are you okay?'

'Oh, yeah! It was fun.' I looked out of the window. Had it been fun? I suppose in some ways it had, in others it hadn't. But maybe that was the gamble you took with casual sex, I thought yet again. You had to take the bad with the good, the sensual with the seedy.

'Yeah, it was fine,' I shrugged.

'Okay ... it's just that it sounds like he got off on controlling you, which isn't very nice,' she wrote back. 'You're not an object there to please him.'

I sat back in my chair, frowning as the bus rattled over a speed bump. With a sigh, I wondered whether she was right. But even if she was and Ollie was 'a bad man', I couldn't deny that he still had a hold on me. He answered something dark inside me: something that wanted to be dominated and snuffed out. If he squeezes too hard and for too long, who cares? a small voice asked. Though it was quiet, it was powerful.

All the same, I told Elle at work that no, I wouldn't be seeing him again. The rational part of my brain was wearing itself thin, repeatedly telling me that it wasn't a good idea. *What if I saw him again and he held onto my throat for even longer?* it asked. And for a while, I did listen.

I began to phase myself out of my WhatsApp conversation with Ollie, but he twigged on. Then came the message that changed my mind; the one which nearly brought me to tears as I left Westbourne Park station one night. *Where did you go? :(,* he asked.

I read that message and felt a lump in my throat. It was so vulnerable, so plaintive. So lonely.

And fuck, I was lonely, too.

As I stepped into the black December evening, I thought about how bereft and empty I felt now that Harry had disappeared from my life. How fucked up I felt after being raped, twice in a year. How messed around and inside out I felt after twelve months of non-stop dating. How tired I was after falling for people and watching the affair fall apart.

Yeah, I was really, really lonely.

Still, Ollie should have been the last person I went to see, right? Why would I go and spend the night with someone who had nearly choked me out in bed? Why would I turn to violence when what I really wanted was comfort?

Looking back, I see that his sadness and neediness attracted mine like a magnet. His loneliness spoke to me in a way no well-meaning friend could. So I lied to them about seeing him again. To explain why I was leaving the flat at 9pm one evening, I made up a different man. I was a terrible liar, however, and failed to give Jen any details.

'Well, at least make sure you meet in public,' she said, looking at me with misgiving.

I told her that I would, then took the tube directly to his flat.

Sitting down on the train to Ollie's, panic began to flutter in my chest. Was I really doing this? I asked myself. Was I really about to spend the night with someone who might kill me, accidentally or not? Staring at my pale reflection in the black window opposite, reality started to close in on me. Was I really going to die tonight? I found myself thinking.

What was more frightening was how little this bothered me. Even more terrifying than that was the flickering hope that it *might* happen. For years, the urge to kill myself had followed me around, tapping me on the shoulder a few times a week. Ignoring that urge had been difficult these past few months, the weight becoming unbearable. I needed a release from it, and if that release meant death … so be it, I thought. The black fog had coated everything by now, cloaking every pinprick of light and making the world feel flat.

There was also a sense of inevitability to all of this which I felt I needed to accept. I'd been the victim of sexual violence multiple times, and this seemed a natural way to finish my life. 'Girl who gets raped' naturally transitions to 'girl who might die'. Perhaps resisting my fate would be even more painful.

More than anything, I was *tired.* So tired. I didn't want to be tired anymore, I decided. I didn't want to fight. I wanted to give in to the pull of the waves, which seemed hell-bent on dragging me under. I wanted to get it over with.

Swallowing and shifting in my seat, I felt tears springing up in the corners of my eyes. I was confused suddenly, my throat catching. No, I was being ridiculous, I began telling myself hurriedly. Ridiculously overdramatic. Of course Ollie wasn't going to kill me that night, and I certainly wasn't going to see him because he might. I liked him and I wanted to see him. That was all. That was all.

Plus, that message ... How could I not see him again after a message like that?

Plugging in my headphones, I pretended that suicidal ideation had nothing to do with my decision. It did a little, though. I'll admit that now.

Ollie stood at his window, watching me amble about in the street below. Citymapper had led me to the row of identical houses, but I couldn't tell which was his.

He laughed when I stepped out of the lift, finally in the correct building and on the right floor.

'That was fun,' he said, pulling me in for a hug.

I pushed him away playfully, in spite of my nerves. My thoughts still jangling, I followed him inside.

Fuck, my heart had been banging on the last leg of the tube journey, but it settled to a quiet patter when we sat down. To my surprise, there was something soothing about his manner this time. He seemed mellow. Looking at me with a pair of tired, concerned eyes, Ollie stroked my arm, telling me about the auditions he'd been to this week. Then he told me I was pretty.

It was strange how this made me feel: both relieved and incredibly, overwhelmingly sad. Maybe he wasn't the monster I'd made him out to be, I thought. Maybe I was safe, and maybe that was exactly what I wanted. I didn't really want to die, did I? Surely not …

We curled up in front of the TV and watched *Hook*, a strange choice for a second-date movie. I didn't mind, though – a glass of wine in hand, his running commentary making me laugh. Settling into the crook of his arm, I closed my eyes from time to time. Looking down at the crown of my head, he said that I reminded him of a cat.

'Not because of your name,' he clarified. 'You're just so cuddly tonight. And I still feel like you might leave me at any moment.'

I chuckled and said that I wouldn't. And I meant it, for the time being. This was all so unexpectedly comforting.

Still, from time to time, sinister comments would trickle in. When we were talking about tattoos, for instance, I said that I wanted one on my wrist but was worried about the pain. Looking at me, he smirked.

'Oh, I think you're alright with pain,' he said, his dark eyes narrowing.

Inevitably, this side of Ollie came to the fore when we returned to the bedroom. He spanked me again, even harder than last time, and I gasped, my skin smarting. With another hand imprinted on my arse, I wondered what was coming next.

It wasn't choking, thank God. We had penetrative sex this time and Ollie came quickly, crumbling down beside me and promptly falling asleep. Almost dizzy with relief, I relaxed into his gentle embrace and closed my eyes.

When I reopened them, he had both hands around my neck. I was vaguely aware that I was dreaming.

Looking up into Ollie's face, I saw an expression that was desperate, panicked. I struggled to make out his words, then realised that he was talking himself into killing me.

'No, I can't … but I have to,' he insisted. 'It's too late now. I've got to do it.'

'No. No, you don't,' I argued calmly. 'Ollie,' I pressed, 'you don't have to kill me.'

He nodded, tears shaking down his face.

'Yes I do, Kitty. Yes, I do.'

'But why?'

'Because I've already killed all of *them*.' He nodded to a heap of indeterminate bodies behind him, and a chill ran up my arms, every hair standing to attention.

When I woke, I realised with a start that he was behind me, winding a leg round mine. It's a strange thing, waking up with the man who's just killed you in your sleep. I wouldn't recommend it.

'You okay?' Ollie murmured. Still covered in goosebumps, I nodded, figuring that I must have jerked both of us awake.

'Yeah. Nightmare,' I whispered back. He mumbled something I couldn't make out and drifted off again.

Wide awake, I stared at the streetlamp outside his window and thought: I have to end this.

———————

Ollie was still half asleep when I left him in the morning.

I kissed him quickly, knowing that it would be the last time. There was no point in lingering.

'Text me later,' he urged me faintly, his mouth half-buried in a pillow.

I said that I would, the words sticking in my throat – I really was no good at lying. Then I picked up my things and walked quietly to the front door, closing it softly behind me.

Down in the lobby, I passed a little girl in a raincoat. She had a sister in an even smaller one, and an irritated father bustling them out the door. She smiled up at me when I held it, and I smiled back, hoping that she'd make better decisions than I did when she was older. That she'd like herself a little bit more.

Then I opened my umbrella and walked away.

———————————◆———————————

Breaking things off with Ollie was easy, in the end. He texted me over Christmas and I replied, not knowing how to end the conversation. Then in January I worked myself up to lie to him (again), saying that I'd rekindled a relationship with an 'ex at home' over the holidays. I don't know if he bought it, but he accepted it.

Okay Kitty, Ollie replied. **Smiley face*. I'm sad but I understand. Hopefully see you again some day.*

My hand shook as I lowered my phone and lay back in my own, safe bed. Staring at the ceiling, I let my thoughts grow quiet, lying there and listening to my heart race.

I'd been so afraid of his response, I realised; so scared that his intensity in the bedroom would translate to viscous anger in the face of rejection. But it didn't, thank God. It didn't.

'Well, doesn't your worry say it all?' Lizzie asked me gently over the phone, days later. 'You were scared of him. That's not right.'

This was true, and a fair point, but it was also an oversimplification. Ollie became a figure of dread for many reasons. There was the dread of what he might do to me, yes, but also the dread of what I might do to myself. It couldn't be healthy, putting yourself into the hands of dangerous people, I thought sadly. It couldn't be normal, hoping that someone might finish you off just to quiet the noise in your head. And yet I'd got on that train knowing that this could happen, even hoping – just a little bit – that it would. I'd sat on the train and I'd got off at his stop and I'd let him buzz me into his flat. A flat I'd nearly passed out in, weeks before.

What was wrong with me? I asked myself. What had happened to my relationship with sex? It had once meant power and liberation; a means to self-realisation. Now it might be my undoing. I knew I was increasingly relying on it to feel nothing, to empty my brain and to escape my cyclical thoughts, but how far would I take this need to be numb? Would I keep re-traumatising myself just so that I didn't have to remember all the other traumas? Would I wind up getting killed in the process?

Passing a hand over my face, I thought: I'm *exhausted.* Then another thought crept into my head. *I miss Harry,* it said quietly.

Oh, I really did. I missed that feeling of connection, those wordless, tender looks. I missed holding his hand and watching him pull a T-shirt over his head in the morning. I missed our long goodbye kisses and the way he rubbed his leg against mine in the middle of the night. I realised I didn't want someone like Ollie, someone who broke me apart. I wanted someone who held me together.

CHAPTER 10

George

I'd self-medicate with sex one final time in 2019. Seven days before Harry reappeared, and seven days before Christmas, I was lonelier than ever. I still had some work to finish up and errands to run, but almost everyone else I knew had left the city, which I roamed like a Victorian ghost, peering into shop windows. And then, as I stood in the fake snow outside Topshop, my phone lit up with a message from George. I'd matched with him an hour ago and, without any small talk, without any pretence of getting to know me first, he asked me what I was doing that night.

'Depends,' I replied. 'What have you got in mind?'

A cocktail bar in Granary Square, he said. Well, that was good enough for me.

My attitude towards sex hadn't changed since dating Ollie. Yes, I wanted someone who puffed me up and made me feel happy and safe and secure, but I didn't see that on the cards. Not after this year. My expectations around sex had plummeted; I didn't need to feel empowered or excited or self-realised, all I needed was to feel *something*. Anything. This blank numbness was killing me.

Crossing the square that night, I glanced over at the fountains, pink water spurting out and slapping the concrete. Stopping, I watched the water turn blue, then green, then orange, and resisted the urge to take my shoes off and run through it, just as a friend had done a year earlier, on a drunken night which ended in ping-pong with strangers.

Pulling my powder-pink coat around me, I clip-clopped over to the bar, using my full weight to open the door. Why do fancy places always have such heavy doors? I wondered. Is it to keep the lean, frail riff-raff out? Tumbling in, I let my eyes adjust to the dim light, taking in the Japanese decor and bespectacled hipsters; the noisy bankers and the waiters wheeling around with small, silver trays. A DJ bobbed along to ambient music in the corner, a glass wall behind him exposing an empty recording booth.

Lord, it was so London. I craned my neck as I looked around, but there was no sign of George.

'Can I help you?' the woman at the podium asked. She had a sleek, dark bob and very narrow glasses. Like an even more glamorous Edna Mode.

'Oh, yes,' I replied in a hushed voice, as if a louder one would reveal that I couldn't afford to drink here. 'Table for two, please.'

Edna led me to a table on the other side of the room, and I sat down to wait, scanning the menu. Fucking hell! This was the sort of place with no happy hour and £15 cocktails. Who was this guy, a banker? I'd have a maximum of two drinks and leave, I decided. It was an expensive time of year.

Another bob-haired waitress returned and took my order, leaving the menu with me in case I wanted to order more. Fat chance of that, I thought.

'Hello,' someone suddenly said, interrupting my internal grumblings. With a start, I looked up to find George in the seat opposite.

Oh, wow. Okay. I hadn't been stunned by his photos, but he was *much* better looking in person. Broad, muscled and compact, he reminded me of a rugby player (and, coincidentally, was also from Rugby). But if he had the body of a bull, he had the face of a bear: all tentative dark eyes and soft, round cheeks; dimples on either side of his mouth. They deepened when he smiled.

'Oh, hello. This is a cool place,' I noted, putting the menu down and hoping he wouldn't notice that I'd ordered the cheapest drink.

'It's alright, isn't it?' George nodded. 'I come here a lot with work.'

'Oh? Where do you work?' Blinking, I realised that I knew absolutely nothing about this man.

'In advertising. It's not what I want to do forever.' He sighed. 'But it *is* good money, I'll give it that.'

'I'll bet.' I blinked again when the waitress arrived with my drink, which was much bluer than I'd been expecting. 'I've spoken to a few people who work in advertising,' I said as she lowered it onto a napkin, 'and there seems to be the general consensus that you've sold your souls to the devil.'

He laughed. 'I guess. But it's not that, I don't mind selling my soul to the devil, if he's buying. It's more just *fucking stressful.'* George stirred his Dark and Stormy with the air of someone who did this a lot, cupping his chin in the other hand. 'I had to fire someone today,' he added, glancing up.

'You fired someone this close to Christmas? Wow. I didn't know I was on a date with Scrooge.'

'Hey, look, it wasn't my choice.' George grinned. 'And it was awful. But *anyway,*' he resumed, straightening his back, 'as I said, I won't be doing this forever.'

'Oh, yeah?' I was grinning now, too, holding my tiny straw between my thumb and forefinger. 'What are you going to do next?'

'Okay, so hear me out.' He paused, glancing up. 'In short, I have this idea for an app.'

I tried not to groan.

'Go on,' I said, attempting a smile, and for the next five minutes he told me about taxis, or savings accounts, or food deliveries, or something. I don't remember what the app was, but I do remember thinking that it already existed. Why was it that women were afraid to ask for a pay rise at work, but men were ready to quit their jobs to design an app already in circulation?

'Sounds like a great idea,' I enthused. 'I'd buy it.'

'Well, great, that's one sale.' George chuckled. 'So what about you, do you want to stay in your job forever?'

I gave him a look.

'Do I want to keep writing SEO articles about pushchairs for the rest of my life?' I paused, finishing my drink. 'No. I'd rather kill myself.'

'Okay,' he laughed again. 'So what's the plan?'

'I don't know.' Musing, I glanced over at the recording booth. 'I think writing, maybe. Journalism? We'll see. I have an interview at *The Times* soon. You never know.'

George nodded, lifting a hand. He asked the waitress if we could get another round of drinks and, in spite of my earlier reservations, I didn't protest.

We drained them in minutes, then ordered a third. Oh shit, I thought. I really can't afford this. But as the Old Fashions flowed, so did the conversation. We sped through topics: where we'd grown up, how many siblings we had, how much we both hated our jobs.

'Fuck it,' I said, four drinks in. 'Sack journalism. I'm going to be a singer.'

'Yeah.' Unsteadily, George lifted his glass. 'And I'm going to make that app, Kitty. You just watch me.'

'Good for you,' I slurred. 'Hey, you know what would be a good idea? An app where you could rate your dates. You know, like Google Reviews? One star: bad. Five stars?' I gave the 'okay' symbol with my hand. 'Five stars: very good.'

'Yes,' George said emphatically. 'Oh my God, that's a great idea. Hey,' he added, looking at me with sudden intensity. 'What would you rate this date?'

I paused in mock thought.

'This date? Mmm. I'd say this date is a solid three.'

'A *three*?'

I chuckled. 'There's still time.'

'Fine, fine. I'll order another round.' He waved a limp hand at the waitress. Again, I didn't protest: I was too far gone now. 'So tell me about your one-star dates,' he grinned when she left.

'No, no.' I waved a hand. 'You first.'

'Alright, fine.' A mixture of emotions passed across George's face. Embarrassment, disgust, then excitement. 'So I went out with this girl. Very good-looking, but she kept disappearing to the bathroom.'

'Oh no. Not a good sign.'

'No. Well, it quickly became obvious that she was doing a *lot* of coke in there.'

'Coke, you say?'

'Coke, I say. And the date just got weirder and weirder. She asked to go back to mine and I said "okay",' he shrugged. 'Because, well, she was a good-looking girl. But when we got in the cab she started um … punching me.'

I stared at him.

'What?'

'Yeah. Just … fists raining down.'

'Fucking hell.' I mouthed around for my straw but missed. For goodness' sake, not this again. 'So what did you do?'

'Kicked her out, of course.' George shifted in his seat, suddenly self-conscious. 'I felt bad, but *I* wasn't getting out of the cab.'

'No, no,' I insisted, waving a hand. 'I think that's fair enough, given that she was beating you to a pulp.'

'And you know what the worst thing was?' George added, looking at me mournfully. 'My Uber rating went right down. From four stars to three.'

I chortled, and he sat a little taller, clearly pleased with this response. 'So go on then,' he prompted, bolstered. 'What was *your* worst date?'

'Oh, I don't know,' I sighed, smiling. 'Probably being grabbed by the throat outside a train station?'

George coughed slightly, midway through finishing his drink. 'Jesus,' he said, putting the glass down. 'What do we do to invite such violence?'

I grinned back at him, impressed with his ability to keep the conversation light. I was having so much fun, talking to him. I was so glad I came.

Inevitably, after that round came another round, and then another one after that. Each time the waitress set one down, we'd shake our heads at the size of the glasses.

'Pitiful,' I spat in response to the fifth.

'I know. Look, I can drink this in four sips,' George said. 'Watch.' He turned the tumbler in his hand, then drank it in one long gulp.

We were like two children at a party, drinking far more squash than was sensible. Sugar coursed through our veins, our knees knocking under the table. Finally, at midnight, we asked for the bill. I paled when it arrived: between us, we'd racked up over £100 in teeny-tiny drinks. This had become a very expensive night, and there was no taking it back now. Suddenly I didn't feel drunk anymore, shocked into sobriety.

Swallowing my remorse, I dug out my debit card.

'No, no. I've got this,' George protested, tapping the machine. I stared at him, my eyes nearly popping out of my head.

'Are you sure?' I baulked.

'Positive,' he replied, his dimples deepening. 'Merry Christmas.'

The rain was pouring outside.

Opening a red umbrella, George pulled me underneath. His eyes were soft when he kissed me, one hand sliding from my waist to my bum. I leaned against his body, warm and firm, and listened to the rain patter around us.

We'd agreed to go to another bar, but found ourselves en route to my flat instead. He held me close while we waited for the Uber, and I clung onto him, trying to ignore the water filling my boots. Finally a bleary pair of headlights appeared, and we tumbled in, still giggling at something or other.

Lord, I feel sorry for that poor driver. As soon as we were on the move, George wound a hand under my skirt, his mouth on my neck. And then, just a few inches behind the silent, stoic man at the wheel, he tried to finger me. Listening to him grunt and groan, I tried not to laugh – baffled as to why he was jabbing my thigh. After a few painful minutes of this I simulated a quiet moan in return, hoping that would satisfy him.

Encouraged by this noise, George grinned down at me. Then, about four centimetres north of my clitoris, he began rotating his thumb in a swirling motion, certain that it was driving me wild. I faked another small groan out of pity.

Still, perhaps things would get better at the flat, I thought hopefully. It was a little awkward back here, there wasn't much room. At last, my building materialised, the blossom tree outside stark and naked in the December night. Thanking the mute, mildly traumatised driver, we clattered out into the road.

'I hope *my* Uber rating hasn't gone down,' I muttered to myself, adding a £2 tip.

George kissed my neck as I unlocked the front door, his hands massaging my waist. He hoisted me up into his arms in the hallway, carrying me towards my bedroom (I directed him with a vague hand). And then he lowered me onto the bed, climbed on top, and resumed the search for my clitoris with the enthusiasm of a leprechaun looking for gold. To our mutual disappointment, he didn't find it.

He did manage to find my vagina, however, and rammed a finger inside in celebration. Clumsily, George proceeded to pour every ounce of energy into ripping me a new one, deciding that finger-blasting me into another dimension was exactly what I needed. I grimaced out of eyeshot. This was the problem with good-looking, charismatic men, I thought: no one told them they were bad in bed. How could you break it to them?

When the finger-blasting became too much, I pushed his hand aside and turned him over. Taking the foreplay into my own hands, I lowered my face to his navel and legs.

George squirmed under my lips, jolting as if electrocuted. When I inched towards his penis, he let out a loud cry.

'Oh my God,' he exclaimed. 'OH MY GOD.'

I bent my head, stifling a burst of laughter. Hesitantly, I continued.

When I *gently* kissed his penis, George let out another shout.

'Yes!' he cried. 'Oh God, oh yes. Oohhhh YE-ES.'

I squeezed my eyes shut, struggling against the mirth rising in my chest. He clawed the sheets, twisting and moaning loudly. Oh, this was too much.

To my disbelief, George only became more and more vocal as the night wore on – every touch sending him into full-volume ecstasy. He gasped and groaned when he was finally inside me, screwing his face into a ball. And then, in a matter of minutes, the whole thing was over.

Flopping down onto the mattress beside me, George panted.

'My God. You've exhausted me,' he declared, running his hands over his face.

I laughed faintly in return, pulling the duvet up to my armpits. What a disappointment! And there had been so much potential, too. Oh well, I thought, turning off the light – it had been worth a try.

In the morning, George suggested that we meet up in the new year.

'Sounds good,' I smiled sleepily, holding the front door open.

'Great.' He returned the smile softly, one hand on the door-frame. 'Have a nice Christmas, yeah? I'll text you?'

'Sure.'

George paused, looking at me. After a few moments he leaned down and kissed me, which was nice. So much nicer than the sex, I thought with remorse. And then, with a final wave, he disappeared down the hall.

Returning to my bedroom and collapsing onto my mangled sheets, I reached for my phone and messaged Lizzie.

Hello, can I come and visit before going home tonight? I asked. *I need to tell you about a guy.*

Sure, she replied quickly. *Who's the guy?*

I'll tell you when I get there, I returned. *But I've had it with men – officially.*

Oh dear, poor George. He'd become the last person I ever ghosted. After some brief chat, I left him on read in favour of Harry, who asked me if I wanted to meet on New Year's Day. Well, we know how that one ended. Serves me right, perhaps.

But, oh, the sex with George *had* been bad, I thought after he left, shaking my head. And the sex did matter. If this past year had taught me anything, it had taught me that.

Chalking it up to another experience, I rolled out of bed and into the shower, washing off the last of my year of casual sex. It had certainly been eventful, I thought as I reached down for the conditioner.

Hours later, I climbed aboard an afternoon train to Bath, where Lizzie now lived. My coffee sloshed around as the carriage began to move, and I looked up at the grey clouds shuffling across the horizon. Soon enough the skyscrapers turned into leafless trees, their branches reaching out for nothing in particular. *Looking forward to seeing you*, I texted Lizzie.

AFTERWARDS

It's been a strange experience, writing this book. At this very
moment I'm sitting in an office chair at a cluttered ladder
desk, my laptop in front of me. Many things have changed.
I don't live in West London anymore; I live with Maisie in
Hackney. Emerald trees line the street, twinkling as the wind
runs through them. Chickens cluck and crow in the garden
next door and an old man potters in and out of their enclosure
every morning, collecting eggs.

I don't write SEO articles about pushchairs anymore,
thank God. I got the job running social media accounts at
The Times and *The Sunday Times*, then moved to *TIME*, where
I'm an Audience Editor (and occasional writer).

None of us work at the start-up anymore, actually. Maisie
and I had Layla and Aisling over for dinner a few nights ago,
and Layla told us about the horrors she sees as a police officer.
Aisling nodded her head as she spoke about the civil service,
where Maisie also works. She's deleted Feeld from her phone,
so I'll never know if 'Gerp' is still active there.

And what of Lizzie? Well, I haven't convinced her to move to London yet. She still lives in Bath, where she picked me up that day in December and took me home to eat a microwave Indian, our forks flying as we complained about men. Speaking of which, she's found a nice one, now: an American who surprises her with flowers and trips away. No more men who message her only to block her; no more talk of galleon cakes.

I'm still depressed. I still have genuine thoughts of suicide, every now and then. The black fog never fully rolls away. It's not nearly as bad as it was when I was seeing Ollie, however: the antidepressants have made the noise grow quieter, and I'm getting free therapy through work. I suppose that most of those therapy sessions will involve talking about what I've written here, in this book. Well, of course they will. I can't believe that I was raped twice in 2019; that I was held by my throat outside a train station and strangled for ten seconds in bed. I still can't believe I had anal sex thrusted upon me with no conversation beforehand.

The truth is: this is the reality of dating. *This.* For most women, casual sex does not equal the zany, consensual escapades seen in *Sex and the City*. As a result, I didn't become Samantha after a year of sexual debauchery; I was broken up and dishevelled by the year's end, convinced that violence was synonymous with sex.

It's uncomfortable to look back on: how much I put up with, how often I'd apply my make up and go to work after being raped or assaulted or bent around in ways I didn't want my body to bend. But why did this have to happen to me? Was I the problem? Did I just have a knack for choosing awful men? Had I been completely unlucky? I wondered this a lot while writing this book, but ultimately came to the conclusion that no, this couldn't be the case. It would almost be comforting if it was, but I know full well that my dating experiences are not unique. They might not have been grabbed outside of train stations or coerced into anal sex, but I've known so many women with at least one story of being assaulted or manhandled or disrespected by a date.

'It's funny,' I said to a friend the other night. 'Imagine if it was par for the course for men to have these experiences.'

She shook her head. 'I can't. If it was, they certainly wouldn't be expected to shrug it off.'

She's probably right.

So, there it is. It's a shame that I wasn't able to have the year of worry-free, empowering sex that I wanted. I feel that regret keenly now, combing back through these chapters. Carefree, casual sex is just one more avenue closed off to women – another part of life we can't see and feel first-hand.

But why is this the case? Why, in a time when we can get more jobs and more independence and more money than ever before, are we denied casual sex without fear? In a post-#MeToo world, why does the threat of rape and assault still chase us everywhere we go?

I don't think dating apps help, with their anonymity and lack of accountability. There's no getting to know each other at work or at a friend's party; no circle of mutual friends who will ask how things are going with you. So people are allowed to commit assault after assault after assault, safe in the knowledge that their family and friends will never find out.

Dating app Bumble started offering free therapy sessions for people who have been sexually assaulted after using its service, which suggests that these apps might feel a sense of responsibility for rising numbers of sexual assault. All the same, why are vicious people *allowed* to exploit these apps to assault and rape women?

Often, women are the ones held responsible for being attacked by people they meet online. We accept that some men will inevitably assault women, and that it's up to the woman to spot this in a man and avoid him; to turn him down before he gets into her bedroom. We're frequently told to be on the look-out; to be careful not to 'put ourselves in dangerous situations'. But the onus should not be on us to avoid sexual assault – the onus should be on men not to assault us. You shouldn't have to get to know a guy before having sex with him, to give him the all-clear before letting him into your bedroom. Firstly, because it's deeply unjust that men can have first date sex with as many women as they like free of fear and anxiety, and we can't. Secondly, because there is no one-size-fits-all for rapists. They're not always frightening men lurking in alleyways or creepy guys hanging around clubs. Sometimes they're clean-cut businessmen or government officials; sometimes they're sensitive academics who claim to be feminists; sometimes they're your boyfriend of six years. So even after all that vetting, a man might suddenly turn on you. You might get raped or strangled or hit against your will, and he's allowed to step out the next morning, whistling as he walks to the station, oblivious to the fact that he's done something wrong. Oblivious or unwilling to acknowledge it, because society certainly doesn't force him to.

And you have to relive that night, again and again and again. You have to cry about it and talk about it and get therapy to banish it from your mind. You have to pay the unnecessary price, which is also financial if you can't get your therapy for free. That's money that could have gone to your health and your happiness, your work or your weekends.

I don't think we can wholly blame dating apps for the insidious problem of rape and sexual assault. People were being raped and assaulted before Tinder and Bumble and Hinge, but the speed with which you can move between partners via the apps puts you at greater risk of being assaulted and raped. The apps may feed into the problem but, importantly, they also expose it.

A wider, more far-reaching problem when it comes to rape and sexual assault is the lack of education about consent. As Soma Sara pointed out in her *Times* interview, many young men use porn to learn about sex, and that is deeply problematic. Ethical, feminist porn does exist, but there's also some very dark pornography out there, and a lack of consent is regularly normalised – even glorified. You can scroll through an endless stream of videos in which women are hurt and humiliated, in which men are aggressive and entitled and physically abusive. The existence of these videos on porn sites suggests that these things are sexy, a turn-on.

This has real-life implications. In defence of porn, it's compared by some to violent video games, the argument being that video games do not make young people more violent, therefore porn does not make them more likely to be sexually abusive. I don't think you can compare the two, however. Much of the violence in video games is enacted in public, and a young person would only have to look outside to see that people do not regularly mow down pedestrians and blow people's heads off. Sex, however, happens in private. A young person might assume that what happens in porn is totally acceptable in real life, that this is 'secretly what women want'.

This is why sex education is so crucial. And yet the only thing I learned in sex ed was how to put a condom on a cucumber. We need to be more rigorous in teaching young people about consent, sexual assault and rape. We need to speak openly about what is and what is not acceptable behaviour.

We need to encourage young men to be compassionate towards women, to see them as human beings.

As it stands, women are routinely raped and assaulted, and it's swept under the rug. Why are we so *okay* with this? As a society, why do we shrug it off? Why is suffering seen as part and parcel of being a woman? It all fits into the overarching structure of the patriarchy; women should be fine with being attacked just as they should be fine with less pay or discrimination at work. Just as they should quietly take the contraceptive pill with all of its side effects; just as they should accept that there is less research into women's health problems. We take on more of the housework when we're mothers. We get shouted at and honked at in the street – sometimes when we're as young as thirteen. But women are meant to take it all on the chin, apparently. When will this change?

It feels particularly important to talk about all of this now. Sabina Nessa was found dead in a park. Sarah Everard was abducted by a police officer, raped and murdered. Young women have been waking up with shooting pains in their legs and gaps in their memories after being spiked by injection at nightclubs. We are living through an epidemic of rape so horrifying that people are being knocked out with needles on dancefloors.

It's difficult to believe that things are getting any better for women. In my bleakest moments, I wonder if they're getting worse. The world certainly seems to be getting smaller and smaller for us. Last night I was on the bus to Camden and felt a sharp pang when I saw a little girl running down the street, her golden hair sent flying. Little does she know that her time to run down the pavement with reckless abandon is running out, I thought.

The whole evening was tinged with irony, I noticed, my heartbeat low and quiet. Here I was on my way to a Laura

Marling gig – something which should have filled me with excitement. Her song 'Master Hunter' had once made me believe that I could sing 'You can get me on the telephone but you won't keep me there', and mean it. That I could enjoy men and leave them with no consequence, no compromise. But I felt sad, looking down at the familiar streets of Chalk Farm and Camden Town, yellow streetlights staring.

During 2019 – that year of supposed self-empowerment – I never quite managed to get the upper hand in my dealings with men. I was never able to feel the lasting control I once imagined to be possible. I was never the hunter; always the hunted.

Such is the case for most women. We don't live in a society hospitable to those who want to feel enduring power and self-ownership. And we're expected to quietly, stoically carry the scars this society inflicts on us, feeling the ramifications of rape years after the event.

After Sarah was murdered, I spoke to two psychologists about my worsening anxiety, and asked whether this was a normal response to a horrific case like hers.

Yes, Dr Emma Svanberg told me. 'If we've had similar experiences, reading stories like Sarah's can trigger our own traumatic memories,' she said.

Dr Chloe Paidoussis-Mitchell agreed. 'When your unconscious mind tells you that you're under threat, it does its job: it tries to keep you alive,' she went on. 'It activates your fight or flight mode and floods you with stress hormones so that you can literally run for your life.

'Once that system is activated, you're in panic mode. Symptoms might include shortness of breath, a tight chest, a hollow feeling in your stomach, shaking, getting a foggy brain, having digestive issues, having intrusive thoughts, feeling overwhelming fear, having difficulty concentrating, not being able to follow a conversation and wanting to withdraw socially. You might feel that you're losing the plot, or that you don't want to connect with your partner.

'And yes, some women will even go so far as to experience symptoms of PTSD.'

'When we feel highly anxious, this can colour our lens of the whole world,' Dr Emma Svanberg adds. 'Often we cope with this by gradually making our comfort zone smaller – for example, only doing things we feel confident doing, or staying close to home.'

Not only that, but feeling permanently unsafe 'affects our memory and concentration. Because our system is so preoc-cupied with keeping us safe, it doesn't have the resources for brain functions such as planning, complex reasoning and lan-guage. We can, as a result, end up making mistakes or doing things that are out of character. This can leave us feeling like there is something wrong with us.'

What struck me during these conversations was how far-reaching the psychological impact of rape and sexual assault is.

So why, as a society, aren't we talking more about the assault on women's mental health, finances and careers, as well as on their bodies? Why are we expecting women to muddle through a state of psychological overload, nurturing everyone else while they feel splintered inside?

Why aren't we dismantling rape culture with a greater sense of urgency? Pain shouldn't be synonymous with the female experience, but we act like it is.

Men: let's take the problem of rape culture off the back burner. Let's pull it down from the shelf and look at it, even though doing so might make you feel uncomfortable. Guilty, even. It may make you feel uneasy, but women are tired of shouldering all this fear and trauma. We're buckling under the weight. We're tired of feeling under siege.

And we are so, so tired of being raped.

One of the most baffling things I realised when writing this book was that many of the men did not think they had done anything wrong. They didn't act like they did, anyway, by requesting further dates and reminiscing on the 'great time' they'd had. Why was Ollie so keen to see me for a second date after acknowledging that he'd strangled me for too long on our first? How did Leo have the gall to mess me about after surprising me with anal sex?

Is misogyny so ingrained that these men didn't care if they made me uncomfortable? Has violent porn convinced them that surprise anal and rough choking is what women want? Is it a matter of cruelty or a matter of ignorance, or both?

Let me be clear when I say that it is men who should be changing the status quo; it is not women's responsibility. But one way we can empower ourselves is by talking about our experiences, insofar as we feel comfortable. Talking is an act of resistance: the patriarchy would like us to suffer in silence; it would like us to keep our trauma to ourselves. It does not want us to speak out against the assaults that broke us apart. So I hope, in a way, this book counts as an act of resistance. And I hope that the more we talk about rape and sexual assault (in its many forms), the less room there will be for men to plead ignorance. No more 'blurred lines' – we're wiping them out.

I've got up now, and I'm walking down the steps into the living room. The leaves outside are in full, green flush, and a blackbird is chirping from one of the branches. The diffuser my boyfriend bought me is trickling away in the background.

I'm grateful to him (not just because of the diffuser, although it is very nice. Ever smelt a mixture of orange and lemongrass? Holy moly). He's taught me that talking things through and asking for permission is normal. He's taught me that I deserve to be treated like a well-rounded and pointy-edged person, worthy of kindness and patience and respect.

Of course, I should have known all of this without him (an inner voice is railing that I shouldn't have had to learn this through a man at all), but in truth, 2019 had shaken my confidence. As the year came to a close, I was no longer sure that I was worthy of anything.

Even so, I'm grateful that year happened. Putting my traumatic experiences aside, I'm glad that I threw myself into a year of casual sex with strangers – for the tender moments and party anecdotes and for showing me that I could, sometimes, find power in sex. Seeing myself in a sexual light was new and thrilling; it was illuminating. It showed me a side of myself I'd never seen before. I was able to kiss and touch and hold people in ways I didn't know I could, after an early experience which made me feel incapable of intimacy. As a result, I had a deeper understanding of myself when I turned 26.

In 2020, the need for temporary pleasure again gave way to a desire for something longer-term, and so, eventually, came Sam. I'm glad that I found his hand at the end of the tunnel. I'm glad that he tells me about his dreams and shows me pictures of his dogs and turns on *Come Dine With Me* while he potters about in the kitchen. I caught my breath the first time he told me that he loved me, just as the sun caught the leaves on my walk home the following day. I'd never felt so happy as I did that morning, smiling up at them.

And now, in the rearview mirror, the ten men become ten memories. Hazy and jagged and sometimes soft. Ten chapters, around 20,000 characters each. Letters on the page.

I've returned to my bedroom window now, my eyes on the sky. The blue has turned to a gentle white, and rain is falling, whispering down through the leaves.